Bc

BOLD ONES
ON CAMPUS

A Call for Christian Commitment

Donald L. Deffner

Publishing House
St. Louis London

The Bible texts in this publication are from the
Revised Standard Version of the Bible, copyright
1946 and 1952 by the Division of Christian Education, National Council of Churches, and are used
by permission.

Concordia Publishing House, St. Louis, Missouri
Concordia Publishing House Ltd., London E. C. 1
Copyright © 1973 Concordia Publishing House

Library of Congress Catalog Card No. 73-78104
ISBN 0-570-03162-1

Manufactured in the United States of America

Rededicated

To Tina (class of '88)

now eight
pigtails bobbing
skipping up a sun-splashed California street
to the school bus
near our home
where the deer and the rattlesnakes play

and who for second grade
composition class
exulted

"I am free!"

Contents

Preface to the Second Edition

Blues, Twentieth Century Blues, are getting me down
Who's escaped those weary Twentieth Century blues?
Why, if there's a God in the sky, shouldn't He grin?
High above this dreary Twentieth Century din,
In this strange illusion, chaos and confusion,
People seem to lose their way.
What is there to strive for,
Love, or keep alive for—say?
Hey, hey, call it a day.
Blues, nothing to win or lose.*

These words of Noel Coward, introducing the original volume of *Christ on Campus,* may have described many a college student a decade or two ago. But not always today.

For far beyond the Unsilent Generation's reaction to the Silent Generation has come the radical, revolutionary, involvement-oriented student of the sixties.

In contrast to the despairing, egocentric tunes of the sixties one student compiled a list of 116 current songs of *affirmation*—not of Christianity, to be sure, but of *positive* values nevertheless—to "love and keep alive for. . . ."

And yet, as a University of Chicago campus pastor noted in the late sixties, "I hope all this

* From "20th Century Blues," by Noel Coward. Copyright © 1931 by Chappell & Co., Ltd. Chappell and Co., Inc., owner of publication and allied rights for the Western Hemisphere. Used by permission.

9

valid concern and activism doesn't fade back into the woodwork and we see the campuses of our land once again become the Halls of Ivy!"

"Little chance!" others might add, as riots and moratoria continue in the environs of academe.

But whatever the cycle — Silent/Unsilent, Activist/Apathete, Reflection/Action — the wheels of State U. grind on . . . And the ongoing questions of life and death, faith and reason, doubt and hope . . . remain.

War, race, drugs, ecology, pollution, eugenics, future shock, space theory, the occult, the Pill, counteracting the Establishment, etc. — these issues and others command the student's attention today as never before. But the perennial, ontological questions continue as well.

As Ellen says in *The Arrangement* (Elia Kazan): "I don't even know who I am!"

It is to the student open to the reexamination of this question that this little volume is addressed.

"People seem to lose their way."

I submit that there is a living, loving, forgiving, contemporary, and discoverable God who wants to show *The Way*.

And I submit that there are still many collegians who are willing to look outside themselves for a vibrant meaning to daily life.

There are still those who have not committed themselves to activism for its own sake, or to the older hoary dogmatisms of relativism, rationalism, empiricism, or the "new humanism." I submit that there are those who in confronting

Christ-men and Christ-women on campus are willing to talk to them—and to "search the Scriptures"—to see if Christ is the Way. There are still students who will grant that it is not the Shepherd who is lost but the sheep—and are open-minded enough to make a systematic examination of the Christian faith and its relevance for their lives.

To repeat, I contend that God *is* a "discoverable God," that He is a "contemporary God," that He is the God manifest in Jesus Christ, who "is before all things" and in whom "all things hold together."

May these pages be but a bridge back to the "Good News for Modern Man"—the Gospels themselves, where students will find God's **answer to the question** *"Who am I?"* For there they will discover the person whom they are to become, and the One who is the Power to be such a "new creation"—our blessed Lord Himself.

So, "come, let us reason together."

A Problem

(First Person: "I just can't *see* it!")

"But the unspiritual man simply cannot accept the matters which the Spirit deals with — they just don't make sense to him, for, after all, you must be spiritual to see spiritual things." (1 Corinthians 2:14 Phillips)

An Insight

(Second Person: "Here, try these glasses.")

"The spiritual man, on the other hand, has an *insight* into the meaning of everything, though his insight may baffle the man of the world. This is because the former is sharing in God's wisdom, and

> Who hath known the mind of the Lord,
> That he should instruct Him?

"Incredible as it may sound, we who are spiritual have the very thoughts of Christ!"

An Affirmation

("Hey! I can *see!* God *is* discoverable!")

"Now, Lord . . . with my own eyes I have *seen* Your salvation. . . ." (Luke 2:29-30 TEV)

A Prayer

("I've just got to tell somebody about this!")

"We cannot stop speaking of what we ourselves have seen and heard."

"Lord . . . allow us, Your servants, to speak Your message with all boldness." (A prayer of the early church, Acts 4:29 TEV)

The Source

(Third Person: "So it happened to you. How do I make the same discovery?")

"They received the Word with all eagerness, examining the Scriptures daily to see if these things were so." (Acts 17:11 TEV)

The Example

(About St. Paul, himself a student)

"For two years Paul lived there in a place he rented for himself, and welcomed all who came to see him. He preached about the kingdom of God and taught about the Lord Jesus Christ, speaking with all boldness and freedom." (Acts 28:30-31 TEV)

The Challenge

(To you)

Speak boldly, and make known the Gospel's secret. You are an ambassador. *Be* bold in speaking the Gospel. (Cf. Ephesians 6:19-20 TEV)

The Bold Date

READ 1 PETER 4

One co-ed was very active in bringing other students to the campus chapel. She always made it a point to speak to her dates about going to church with her.

One week she had a date on a Tuesday night and in the course of the evening invited the young man to come to church with her on the following Sunday. He agreed to come.

On Friday night the young lady was out with a different young man, and in the course of the conversation she also invited him to come to church with her on the following Sunday.

It wasn't until Saturday morning, however, that she realized she had a social problem on her hands. So she phoned the campus pastor and said, "Pastor, you got me into this jam, now you get me out!"

But the campus pastor thought this was a very delightful kind of jam to get into and said, "Well, why don't you bring both of them?"

She did. Both young men appeared in church with her, one sitting on each side. Both eventually became members of the congregation. One of them was killed in naval action during the war.

Another girl in a similar situation got out of it another way. She attended the early service with one student and the late service with the other, neither of the two interested young men knowing about the other.

Then she told the pastor, "If I didn't like coming here, it wouldn't have been so easy. As it was, I really enjoyed it."

So often the subject of religion, particularly one's own personal credo, is the last thing that is the subject of conversation on a date.

But the Scripture is clear that the Christian is ready to speak of his faith at all times: "Always be prepared to make a defense to anyone who calls you to account for the hope that is in you, yet do it with gentleness and reverence." (1 Peter 3:15)

Indeed, one is not only to defend his faith, but he should not be able to keep silent about "the things that he has seen and heard."

Have you joined the "secret service"? Do you "keep quiet about it"? Or are you a gentle and reverent witness to the "faith that is in you"?

The Identity Crisis

READ PSALM 16

We were sitting at LaVal's Pizzeria one-half block from U.C. — Berkeley. The Cal student next to me mused: "What disturbs me most is the increasing polarization between different groups in society about the issues we should be working on together. There's a growing anti-intellectualism . . . science and technology vs. the common man. Growing protests *against* ecological concerns, pollution control. I hear increasing cries: 'You're infringing on my personal rights as to what I can and cannot do!'"

Another added: "And just where do I fit in all this? Social and political inequities . . . the questions I have about the whole process of formal education . . . relating to the cultural values of the day . . . the *why* of things . . . finding a *rationale* for what we do . . . ."

As Ellen said in *The Arrangement:* "I don't even know who I am . . . ."

What's the question? The *first* question, that is. Isn't it again the question of man — who he is, where he is going, and why?

Alvin Rogness tells the story of a boy on his bicycle hit by a car. When we hear about the accident, is our first question, "What happened to the bike?" or "What happened to the boy?"

Which is more important — "The Age" or *you*?

As we face the crises which refuse to go away: war, racism, drugs, a shaky economy, etc., the real question is: Do we see these problems only horizontally or vertically, with only an earthly dimension or *sub specie aeternitas*—in the light of eternity?

Do we rely on God's grace in Christ to supply our need? That doesn't mean we are any less concerned about any dilemma facing our society. We work just as hard at the problems, but we rely on our Lord through His means of grace instead of our own clever minds.

As Thomas Merton writes in *The Seven Story Mountain:* "[God] is much more anxious to take care of us, and capable of doing so, than we could be ourselves. It is only when we (both individually and as a people or society in history) refuse His help, resist His will, that we have conflict, trouble, disorder, unhappiness, ruin."

Who are you? What's the—*is* there—a purpose in life?

Martin Luther King Jr. stated: "I still believe that standing up for the truth of God is the greatest thing in the world. This is the end of life. The end of life is not to be happy. The end of life is not to achieve pleasure and avoid pain. The end of life is to do the will of God, come what may."

The Age of Aquarius

READ REVELATION 22

"Tina, look! There on TV! Just think! Those are live pictures of men walking on the moon!"

To which she ho-hummed in response: "Look, Dad, after all, it *is* Apollo 16!"

To my 7-year-old it was just *another* moon shot. How times have changed!

"It's the Age of Aquarius! A new era of peace, love, joy is being ushered in!"

I'll buy that—and work for it, too.

"Of course, it's a new age in morals, too. The family must go. God is dead. The church is irrelevant. We must destroy those institutions which ..."

Wait a minute! One change at a time!

Of course, change doesn't wait. It *comes.* Hurtles at us. And we aren't at all prepared for this "Future Shock," says Alvin Toffler.

But what bothers me are those students who have read works like Toffler's—and heard similar predictions—and accepted them *uncritically.*

Does the Christian just float along with the stream—culturally and morally—and say blandly: "Well, I guess that's the way it's going to be"? Or does he *resist* it—when the social drift is *not* in keeping with The Way of our Lord Jesus Christ?

As Paul charged: "Don't let the world around you squeeze you into its own mould, but let God re-mould your minds from within, so that you may prove in practice that the Plan of God for you is good, meets all His demands and moves towards the goal of true maturity." (Romans 12:2 Phillips)

Let's take another look at the culture around us. I don't think we have the "New Age" with us yet. As Harvard sociologist Pitirim Sorokin said, all the elements of moral decay in the Roman Empire a generation before its fall are present in our country today.

Remember them—in Edward Gibbon's great work *Decline and Fall of the Roman Empire?*

1. The rapid increase of divorce; the undermining of the dignity and sanctity of the home, which is the basis of human society.

2. Higher and higher taxes and the spending of public moneys for free bread and circuses for the populace.

3. The mad craze for pleasure, sports becoming every year more exciting and more brutal.

4. The building of gigantic armaments when the real enemy was within: the decadence of the people.

5. The decay of religion—faith fading into mere form, losing touch with life and becoming important to warn and guide the people.

Truly, we are a nation that has forgotten how to blush (Jeremiah 6:15)!

But we are a nation to which the God over all ages past and those to come calls out:

"Obey My voice, and I will be your God, and you shall be My people; and walk in all the ways that I command you, that it may be well with you." (Jeremiah 7:23)

The *Age of Aquarius?*

Or the ageless Christ for an aging and agonizing world?

What is your choice?

Love, Not Haight

READ ECCLESIASTES 12

Have you "been there"? Haight-Ashbury a few years ago. Any number of its counterparts today.

And seen the once pretty young girl literally lying in the gutter on a trip, her "boy friend" unable to get her drugged body on its feet?

Says one young girl:

"I'd like to talk about drugs for a while. Now *I've been there* and to anyone out there wondering 'what'll it do to you?' I'm a perfect example of it. I have mentally killed myself. I started out differently from others — at least some others. I started out on pills, ups, downs, anything that would get me high. So now I've graduated from pills. And my friends said, 'Aw, come on! Come with us. Do it!' So I smoked grass, hash. I swore I'd never do anything else. Then I got a little more daring. I said, 'What the hell — nothing will happen to me.' Then I took acid. And when I went to speed, I knew I was finished. So I got help. Slowly but surely, I'm coming back to reality. But I don't know if I'll ever be the same."

And a co-ed wrote:

"I was impressed with acid because I felt so enlightened. My eyes were finally opened, I believed. And then I started doing a lot of speed in order to make it through my first year of college. I began to rely on it to get papers written and to study for exams. I thought it was great — the only answer. I did well, and so I persisted on doing more and more speed. Then I began to notice that my memory was failing me. It was exasperating and extremely frustrating, for I found myself forgetting insane little things—where I had put books and numerous other objects. I would recall conversations with people, but my concept of time was failing, and I could not remember when I had the conversations—a day or a week ago.

"I feel now that drugs tend to make the individual rationalize, and they hinder him from attaining a true balance with the various aspects which constitute life itself! I've now learned that one can easily come to terms with the universe, without any aid of drugs. It is a question of how strong one's character is. Nobody wants a crutch in order to 'make it,' and what are drugs but a crutch? A person can use the drug or the drug can use the person, and unfortunately most people are used by the drug."

"Don't you know that your body is the temple of the Holy Spirit, who lives in you, the Spirit given you by God? You do not belong to yourself but to God; He bought you for a price. So use your bodies for God's glory." (1 Corinthians 6:19-20 TEV)

A 17-year-old boy who had pleaded guilty to possessing hallucinogenic drugs was being sentenced by the judge. "Do you know who is going to serve that year?" he asked. "Not you; your mother and father will serve that year. That is what's wrong. They get sentenced. They get sentenced for a lifetime. You serve a year. Your body is in the stockade for a year, but their souls are tormented for a lifetime. Why? Because you are a selfish, spoiled boy, that's why."

The judge went on to point out to the boy that his doctor wasn't on drugs, nor his lawyer. His astronauts, President, legislators weren't. Nor the engineers who build the bridges, roads, planes, and autos he uses.

"None of them have been on drugs, and this is because of people like your mother and father.

"But in the world of the future the same may not be true. Teachers, doctors, lawyers, legislators — products of the new drug-oriented generation — may well be high as kites.

"You won't know whom to send your child to, or whom to trust your life to.

"Let's see what kind of world you leave to your children," he concluded, "before you talk about the world that we left to ours." *

*"All these things happened to them as examples for others, and they were written down as a warning for us. For we live at the time when the end is about to come.

"The one who thinks he is standing up better be careful that he does not fall. Every temptation that has come your way is the kind that normally comes to people.

"For God keeps His promise, and He will not allow you to be tempted beyond your power to resist; but at the time you are tempted He will*

* Augsburg Publishing House, Minneapolis, Minn.: *Tomorrow Is a Handful of Together Yesterdays,* John Rydgren. 1971.

give you the strength to endure it, and so provide you with a way out.

"So then, my dear friends, keep away from the worship of idols . . . ." (1 Corinthians 10:11-14 TEV)

Idols such as alcohol, pot, amphetamines, speed, acid, moon, mesc, joy powder, etc., etc., etc.

"Down with the Establishment!"

READ EPHESIANS 6

"I'm going over and pick up my unemployment check. Then I'll drop in at the university to see what's holding up my check for my federal education grant. After that I'll pick up our food stamps. Meanwhile you go over to the free clinic and check your tests, pick up my new glasses at the health center, then go to the welfare department and apply for another increase in our eligibility limit.

"Then I'll meet you at 5 o'clock at the federal building for the mass demonstration against the rotten Establishment."

Not all students would see the above scene as either humorous or self-contradictory. Feeling that society — that is, all of us — owes to each person the dignity and the right of a livelihood, there should still be the freedom to criticize those institutions which dehumanize and exploit the individual.

Down with the Establishment!

Parents, too, come under fire as authority-figures symbolic of much that is wrong with the status quo.

"Dad, would you for just once tell me why you think it's wrong for me to smoke pot when you've been through a pack of cigarettes already today, and now you're on your second cocktail?"

How do we live with each other — father, mother, son, daughter — when from our perspective we see an obvious hypocrisy, or at least a duplicity and double standard which we just can't stand?

In *Last Summer* Rhoda is encouraged by the little clique of David, Peter, and Sandy to tell of some horrible incident in her past. Finally, painfully, she tells of how her mother drowned while trying to win a stupid $10 bet at a boring cocktail party, and how later she had spat on her mother's grave.

"When everyone else had left, I stayed behind and spat on her grave because she had no right to die that way, no right to leave me all alone...."

Does that tragic scene grab you as it does me? Whatever her mother's failings, she was still Rhoda's *mother*. And she owed the orphaned 10-year-old a *mother*.

Whoever, whatever else I am, I owe my four children a loving father. I am not my own person. I owe all I am and have to God. And I have distinct obligations to all those around me.

You know, it works the other way, too. "She had no right ...." You and I have no right to cheat our parents of respectful, loving children — even when we disagree with them, or when communication has completely broken down.

In *Before They Start to Leave: Guidelines for Parents of Teenagers* (Concordia) Walter Riess states that in many instances communication and reconciliation can only take place when — both admitting complete defeat and their mutual, utter sinfulness before God — there can be the divinely-empowered miracle of forgiveness and a new relationship with God's love at the center of it.

We may still not "agree" with each other, but by God's grace we can "accept" each other, even as He has accepted us, the "unacceptable," and grow towards an increasingly mature understanding between each other.

Even as God's mercies to us are "new every morning," so mutual forgiveness — and then communication — *are possible* each day the Lord lets us live.

Remember?

"Thou shalt honor thy father and thy mother, that it may be well with thee and thou mayest live long on the earth.

What does this mean? We should fear and love God that we may not despise our parents and masters, nor provoke them to anger, but give them honor, serve and obey them, and hold them in love and esteem."

As God has loved us, let us love one another. (1 John 4:11)

"Above everything, love one another earnestly, for love covers over many sins." (1 Peter 4:8 TEV)

"Get a Marriage License? — That's a Scrap of Paper!"

READ EPHESIANS 5

"We love each other and we're promised to each other. So we're really married in God's eyes — right? So why get that scrap of paper at city hall? I'm under God's law first, not the state — right? Besides, we don't like the governor of this state!"

How do you feel about that point of view? Beyond pointing to the countless persons I've known who used that "married in God's eyes" line to sleep with their girls or fiancees and then later dropped them flat, how does one cope with such rationalizations?

That's what it really is, you know — *rationalization* — which by definition is an attempt to justify that which one knows *to be wrong.*

Why wrong?

First of all, *if* we are talking from a Christian point of view, why doesn't a Christian cheerfully desire to obey "the existing authorities . . . put there by God" (Roman 13:1 ff. TEV), including the state requirement for a marriage license, since this does not defy God's law (Acts 5:29)? "Render unto Caesar . . ." said our Lord.

O. K. So the state does recognize common-law and other types of relationships in certain circumstances. Is that God's — or even the state's — ideal?

"And you shall not walk in the customs of the

28

nation which I am casting out before you; for they did all these things, and therefore I abhorred them." (Leviticus 20:23)

Why do you want marriage without its legal sanction *and responsibilities* (involving such factors as concern for children and their legal protection, etc.)?

For some, the rationalization stems from "the illusion of the isolated individual."

Not long ago Dr. Robert Elliot Fitch, dean of Pacific School of Religion in Berkeley, wrote a classic article in *The Christian Century* titled: "A Common Sense Sex Code." It caused such a shock wave when it hit the presses that requests for reprints in the tens of thousands came in. (Look it up in the library: Oct. 7, 1964, pp. 1233-35.)

In the piece, written from a pragmatic, humanistic point of view (which complements — is not antithetical to — the Biblical!) Christian theologian Fitch recalls the ironic contradiction between the experience and the creed of a young social worker in defense of her client.

"But of course it's nobody's business but hers! Nobody else's business — when a clergyman, a social worker, a legal officer, an adoption agency, foster parents and, in this instance, a good piece of the machinery of the United States government were involved in cleaning up the mess! But, says someone, let us leave out the baby. Very well, then, leave it out (when you can). The social consequences of the sexual intimacies of two persons are still enormous in extent . . . .

"Love may be initiated by two private individuals, but it is *in effect* a public transaction which must meet social standards."

O. K. So you say you are not "hiding anything." Many of your friends are doing the same thing.

But what is the result?

Another fallacy surfaces at this point — presuming you're not concerned about the effect unmarried parents have upon a child.

"But we're waiting to have children," you may say.

Well, what kind of contraception are you using?

If it's the pill — beyond the long range results of its use, which are still in doubt — who's kidding whom?

"Personal responsibility has not disappeared because now you can depend on the pill," says Dr. Fitch. "There may be an infallible pill, but, as every doctor knows, there is no such thing as an infallible patient. The proportion of persons with enough disciplined regularity of habit to take a prescribed pill at the specified time, without fail from day to day, is scarcely as much as one in 25. When impulse and passion are mingled with the business, then the proportion must be even lower. And in this sort of a thing, a miss is as good as a mile."

In fact, Dr. Margaret Mead (remember *Coming of Age in Samoa* in Soc. 1?), who several years ago recommended legalization of childless trial "marriages," has completely reversed herself.

Note that she does not speak as a Christian but as a humanistic anthropologist:

"If you want the experience of full-time companionship with someone you love—and this is what you should want, for it is the most satisfactory and fully responsible relationship—you had better get legally married, use contraceptives responsibly and risk divorce later. You are risking even more if you don't."

Here is a point where many intellectuals of our day, be they pragmatic humanists or Christians, are in complete concurrence.

Sexual control before marriage, respect for legal marriage, and the cruciality of the family as the primary unit in the raising of children and as the root of a stable society—these are hardly unique to the Christian world view!

So *Future Shock* Toffler predicts the modular family, and others point to a variety of emerging nonmonogamous, nonnuclear "family" life styles. Do we like sheep follow cultural sociological patterns, or do we ask:

"What is God's desire—not my own—for my relationship with my spouse, and God-willing, my children?"

Try Ephesians chapter five again. Read it in Today's English Version—*Good News for Modern Man.*

Still think "it's nobody's business but ours!"?

What do those outside the church think of your "marriage in God's eyes"?

Keep in mind that verse in 1 Thessalonians 5:22: "Abstain from all *appearance* of evil."

I have a son and three daughters. You know, I couldn't say to any one of them: "You don't feel like a legal ceremony? It's O. K. Go ahead. Live together. You have Mother's and my blessing. There'll be no shame. No guilt."

Could you say that to your daughter?

"Ho! Ho!" says the cynical voice from the rear of the room.

"*You* put that shame and guilt there! If we can just get rid of the sexual hang-ups still slopping over into this Aquarian Age from Victorianism, we'll be free!"

Good comment!

Are the feelings there because of Queen Victoria or because *that's the way God meant man*—not even uniquely *Christian* man—*to be*?

"Since you are God's dear children, you must try to be like Him. Your life must be controlled by love, just as Christ loved us and gave his life for us, as a sweet-smelling offering and sacrifice which pleases God. Since you are God's people, it is not right that any questions of immorality, or indecency, or greed should even be mentioned among you . . . .

"You may be sure of this: no man who is immoral, indecent, or greedy (for greediness is a form of idol worship) will ever receive a share in the kingdom of Christ and of God.

"Do not let anyone deceive you with foolish words: it is because of these very things that God's wrath will come upon those who do not obey Him. So have nothing at all to do with such people. You yourselves used to be in the darkness, but

since you have become the Lord's people you are in the light.

"So you must live like people who belong to the light. For it is the light that brings a rich harvest of every kind of goodness, righteousness, and truth.

"Try to learn what pleases the Lord. Have nothing to do with people who do worthless things that belong to the darkness. Instead, bring these out to the light." (Ephesians 5:1-3, 5-11 TEV)

Politics and Pluralism

READ PROVERBS 4

"My, you're dogmatic!" said the student.

"Who isn't?" replied the other.

Whether one is "far left," "far right," "middle of the road," "uninvolved," "a political skeptic," or what, he is "dogmatic," that is, committed to that point of view. Even the one who is committed to *changing* his point of view is doctrinaire in *that* stance!

A politically conservative student at the University of California was quoted in the *San Francisco Examiner-Chronicle* as saying he found the Berkeley scene as "intolerably leftist-oriented." He said it was "the most stifling intellectual atmosphere possible" and said of his profs that "with rare exceptions, they ridicule any other idea except for the far left." Of his peers: "They seem to accept leftist politics without question."

The extreme result of such rigidity was described by the "Berkeley bomber," who said: "I cut off ties with moderates, liberals, anyone who didn't agree with me totally. It's so easy to resign yourself to violence as the only effective way to combat a system you conceive to be fascist. Once you're committed to violence, you reinforce your own militance by shutting off all other viewpoints. You won't hear other people; you can't hear other people. The ties you establish with fellow revolutionaries bind your mind to the ethic of violence. By the time fall rolled around, I was ready to take violent action."

Where are you on the political spectrum? How "opinionated" are you? Are you open – or do you at least listen – to another point of view?

Can the church validly be *pluralistic,* that is, be a fellowship of those with radically disparate political points of view?

A statement by representatives of the Lutheran Council in the U. S. A. on the reconciliation of division on the war issue has affirmed that "reconciliation is fundamental to the Christian life and that forgiveness is central to the meaning of Christ's life, death, and resurrection," and that the concern of the churches must be for "understanding, acceptance, and reconciliation among Americans who disagree about the war."

The statement called for acts of reconciliation between those who believe they served their nation by supporting this war and those who believe they served . . . by refusing to support it; loving concern for those participants who now return to a society which may forget their service or give it a negative meaning, and for those who refused to participate for reasons of conscience.

Do you buy such pluralism?

How does that other person differ from you in his political stance, his obnoxious manner of expressing his convictions, his life-style, his dress, his hair length (long *or* short), or whatever?

"I may have all knowledge and understand all secrets; I may have all the faith needed to move mountains – but if I have not love, I am nothing. . . . Love is patient and kind; love is not jealous, or conceited, or proud; love is not ill-mannered, or selfish, or irritable; love does not keep a record of wrongs . . . . For our gifts of knowledge and of inspired messages are only partial; but when what is perfect comes, then what is partial will disappear." (1 Corinthians 13:2, 4-5, 9-10 TEV)

The Solution to Pollution

READ PSALM 24

The cartoon depicted two Martians in outer space arguing vehemently. Finally the one in utter disgust said to the other: "Oh, go to earth!" The comment isn't so funny when we consider the dire state of our globe, where we are "standing knee deep in refuse, shooting rockets to the moon."

There is the pollution of the sea. Says Stanford biologist Paul Ehrlich: "No one knows how long we can continue to pollute the seas with chlorinated hydrocarbon insecticides, polychlorinated biphenyls and hundreds of thousands of other pollutants without bringing on a worldwide ecological disaster."

It is an idle hope, accordingly, to feel that sea-farming can feed the double-the-present 3½ billion people who may inhabit the earth in 30 to 40 years.

Air pollution is already incredible, with contamination reported even at the North Pole and at Antarctica.

Watershed and river pollution . . . noise pollution . . . one could go on and on. We have only seen the "tip of the iceberg."

To meet this crisis vast programs of political and social action have been set into gear. Action is needed, to be sure. But is this basically a political or an ethical/theological problem?

The real issue has to do with man's very

reason for his existence and his relationship with his fellowman.

In short, the problem is *man himself.*

As one analyst notes, Americans consume three times more food than the masses in South America. Annually we each discard 2,500 pounds of waste. *Our guilt is overwhelming.*

So if we're talking about guilt, *the issue is ethical.*

As Martin Allan Jackson has said: "Who would give his neighbor's children untreated sewage to drink? Who would pipe the pollutants from his car's exhaust into his living room or nursery?

"If I love my neighbor as I love myself I shall do what is good for him . . . ."

So the "solution to pollution" is found in the religious sphere—love, not just "Action!"

So that we can really sing again:

This land is your land, this land is my land
From California to the New York Islands. . . .

How about a career in ecology? There's a crying need for ecological experts by the thousands right now.

How about a full-time career in "love thy neighbor"?

Now let's have some action!

Are Horoscopes Harmful?

READ MATTHEW 4

"Hey, Dad, did you know Jesus was a Capricorn?" said the preacher's daughter to her surprised father.

Everywhere in the past few years—even inside the church (!)—has come a renewed interest in astrology, the occult, the transcendental. Stroll down Telegraph Avenue in Berkeley and shop after shop is filled with zodiac charts, books on I Ching, ESP, PK, tarot cards, and other aspects of "The New Spiritualism." And across the Bay in San Francisco Anton Levy begins another black mass in his Church of Satan, a young woman lying naked on a red fur-draped altar while he intones: "*Say* your hates and lusts!" "May all your lustful thoughts reach fruition!"

And one critic, discussing William Blatty's *The Exorcist,* mused: "God is dead. Christ is a commodity. Political and moral leaders are invisible. The only one left with even a touch of glamour seems to be Satan."

What attitude does the Christian take towards all this? Are horoscopes harmful? Are seances sinful? Are Ouija boards really witchcraft?

Scripture makes it very clear that evil—and its personification in the devil—is real. As one pastor put it: "Followers of occultism and other Satanic doctrines may be 'sincere,' but they are *sincerely wrong.* The Bible warns us against sorcerers, witchcraft . . . and devils."

Satan is mentioned 35 times in the New Testament, how he opposes God, tests Christ (Matthew 4:10), leads the kingdom of evil (Matthew 12:26), tempts Peter to rebuke Christ, (Matthew 16:23), seduces Judas (Luke 22:3) and Ananias (Acts 5:3), and causes disease (Luke 13:16). *He* has been defeated (Luke 10:18), but he still tries to defeat *us.* (2 Corinthians 2:11)

Scripture's words are right to the point: "For we are not fighting against human beings, but against the wicked spiritual forces in the heavenly world, the rulers, authorities, and cosmic powers of this dark age. So take up God's armor now! Then when the evil day comes, you will be able to resist the enemy's attacks, and after fighting to the end, you will still hold your ground." (Ephesians 6:11-12 TEV)

The question then is: "Why 'go to the devil'?" "Why 'go to hell'?"

Why not go to Christ? *He* is the One who says: "Don't be afraid! I am the First and the Last. I am the Living One! I was dead, but look, I am alive forever and ever. I have authority over death and the world of the dead." (Revelation 1:17-18 TEV)

One more thought. Commenting on the renascence of interest in the occult, sociologist Fr. Andrew M. Greeley states: "What is going on is authentically, if perhaps transiently and bizarrely, religious . . . it's the new pursuit of the sacred. It is so funny, and yet so serious. Students cannot talk about it without laughing, and yet they must interrupt their laughter to protest that they respect the goals of the new devotees of the sacred . . . ."

Christians should see a vast open door for the Gospel in this renewed interest in the transcendental. Those stargazers who have been disillusioned or disenchanted by Christians who have *not* evidenced a living, dynamic witness to a very much alive and contemporary God can yet be challenged by you and me. We direct them not to the "works of darkness" but to "seeking those things which are above."

We must direct them to a living Christ who conquered the powers of death and hell by His victory on the cross and in the tomb, and who is seen in our lives as the only answer to the evil of sin and death that still plague us every day.

"Oh, Lord, revive Thy church, beginning with me!"

The Activists Are the Apathetes

READ PROVERBS 3

The mother glowered at her teen-age daughter sitting sullenly on the floor.

"You know what you are?" she screamed at her. "You're apathetic! *Apathetic,* do you hear! You know what that means, don't you?"

"I couldn't care less," responded the girl with a sigh.

My Graduate Theological Union class "Reaching the Educated Adult" had not started yet. We were meeting at the Franciscan School of Theology, two blocks from the Cal campus, and demonstrations were scheduled for noon at Sather Gate.

"I hope we're having class today," said the one intense M. A. candidate who had arrived early. I affirmed that we were, and he continued: "I had some of my best classes at Santa Barbara while the Bank of America was burning."

This young scholar (by year's end he was already asked to teach a course next fall alongside his graduate studies) was a "radical" politically, but refused to waive his academic responsibilities for a campus shut-down to go on another Berkeley window-breaking spree.

President W. Allen Wallis of the University of Rochester has stated that if there are to be activists and others who purport to have answers to social problems, then they should "spend at least as much time and effort in learning what man already knows and has already tried as do those who are would-be executives, or physicists, or physicians."

He states: "It is among the students so often called apathetic that we find those who are truly concerned and truly committed. It is to this great majority of truly concerned and truly committed students . . . that we may confidently look for future leaders who have, in Ortega's words, 'high creative passion . . . with the constancy of clear understanding and a calm will.'"

And in the *Washington Post* Jack Valenti describes the "Vanishing American"—the trained professional who "invests every task or duty, no matter how small, with discipline of mind and spirit."

He recalls meeting the late Babe Didrikson Zaharias, the legendary woman athlete at a golf clinic once, and asking her: "How can I learn to hit a golf ball the way you do?"

"Simple," she said, laughing. "First you hit a thousand golf balls. You hit them until your hands bleed and you can't hit any more. The next day you start all over again, and the next day and the next. And, maybe a year later, you might be ready to go 18 holes. After that you play every day until the time finally arrives when you know what you are doing when you hit the ball."

Valenti lauds the ideas of many youths, but notes the difficulties in desiring "instant fulfillment" and demanding: "Adopt *my* views *now!*" The problem: too many of them are *not prepared*.

"Let me sit in a discussion where decisions are to be made and I can quickly and accurately point out the professionals. They know the issues, have untangled the crossing threads of logic and reaction, understand the facts cold, and can, because they have done the necessary homework, come up with suggestions that may lack passionate intensity but usually make the most sense . . . .

"I would count the foremost asset of a respected man to be that discipline of self which instructs him in the knowledge of his craft. This means a dedication and a work schedule that sometimes can be rather dismaying. Still, there is no other way to acquire that standard of excellence which is the mark of the professional and the major specification for achievement."

"Study to show thyself approved unto God, a workman that needeth not to be ashamed, rightly dividing the Word of truth." (1 Timothy 2:15 KJV)

Are You the "Independent Type"?

READ PSALM 36

"I swear—by my life and my love of it—that I will never live for the sake of another man, nor ask another man to live for mine."

So states John Galt in Ayn Rand's *Atlas Shrugged*. Ayn Rand (also author of *The Fountainhead*) espouses "objectivist ethics," which stresses individualism to the nth degree.

There are some siren-like appeals in her "new" morality of intellectual self-interest. But as Charles Frederick Schroder says in *The Christian Century* article "Ayn Rand: Far-Right Prophetess": "Granting her assertion that pride in one's productivity and personal accomplishments is highly desirable, let us not forget—as she evidently has forgotten—that personal pride easily degenerates into mere vanity. We must not underestimate the importance of initiative and independence of mind, but at the same time we must realize that in the complex society of today men are necessarily *interdependent* as well. Let us hope that these new prophets of the right will not lose sight of the fact that Christian social responsibility demands that no man be an island."

How independent a person are you?

Canon Bryan Green suggests that everything we do has societal implications. "The only *private* thing you can do is die!" he asserts. And someone else has noted that even communes cut off from society only last an average of 18 months. Ultimately structures develop, and the need for relation to the rest of society becomes increasingly pressing.

We need each other.

Listen to the words of Simon and Garfunkel's *I Am a Rock* once again. Does the person in that song *want* help? Or is he just crawling back into his little box—away from people? He has been hurt by life, no doubt, and needs our love and reaching out to him.

But how quickly "I am a rock . . . I am an island" can degenerate into a tragic egotism and masochistic self-pity.

On July 4, 1972, Reverend Roy C. Nilsen, in summer school at Pacific Lutheran Seminary, sat atop the Berkeley hills, and looking out at the Golden Gate across the Bay, penned these words:

Celebration

Isn't it funny how we celebrate independence—
But no one celebrates dependence!
We mock it—we scorn it—
We say, "To be dependent is to be weak."
Would the flower mock the stem,
Or the leaf the branch,
Or the oxygen the air?
Man is a sad creature:
Claiming to be wise, he is foolish:
Desiring to be free—
He is bound to the fetters of self.
His independence is as a chain that binds him
And his celebration—a sham.
For one can only celebrate life—dependently—
In him who is Life Abundant.

"Go Tell It on the Mountain"

READ ACTS 17

In *Lutheran Education* Martin L. Koehneke tells of the significant contributions made to the work of the Red Cross by the black physician and scientist Dr. Charles Richard Drew.

While working on a D. Sc. degree at Columbia University he wrote a dissertation on "banked blood." He later developed techniques for separating and preserving blood and contributed significantly to blood plasma research.

His work received international recognition, and he was invited to London to set up the British Blood Bank. He also directed the Red Cross blood donor project in World War II. It is impossible to calculate the millions of lives saved as the direct result of his work.

"His life ended tragically in an auto crash on April 1, 1950, at the age of 46. His life might have been saved if he could have been admitted to the all-white hospital that had a blood bank. The black hospital did not have one . . . ."

"Sorry about that, Charles!"

Pater, peccavi . . .

In "Toward a Black Psychology" (*Ebony,* Sept. 1970) Dr. Joseph White, black professor of psychology and director of the Black Studies Program at the U. of California at Irvine, states: "We have worked in the fields from sun up to sundown, laid rails, picked cotton, scrubbed floors, messed with chain gangs, reared other people's children and at the end of three centuries have very little to show for this monumental effort at hard work."

"Sorry about that, Joseph!"

Pater, peccavi . . .

In *Go Tell It on the Mountain,* James Baldwin's powerful novel which gives such penetrating insights into the black religious experience, young John wanders out of Central Park onto Fifth Avenue and admires the old-fashioned horse carriages lined along the curb. He watches the horses, "enormous and brown and patient, stamping every now and again a polished hoof," and dreams of what it would be like to have one day a horse of his own.

And he envisions having his own home, a beautiful wife, admiring children for whom he would buy electric trains. And there would be turkeys and cows and chickens and geese and other horses, and a closet full of whiskey and wine . . . .

Straight ahead, down Fifth Avenue, he watches the graceful women in fur coats who look into the windows that hold silk dresses and watches and rings. "And what were their houses like when in the evening they took off these coats, and these silk dresses, and put their jewelry in a box, and leaned back in soft beds to think for a moment before they slept of the day gone by?"

"Sorry about that, James!"

Pater, peccavi. . . .

Dietrich Bonhoeffer said: "To serve our brother, to please him, to allow him his due and let him live is the way of self-denial, the way of the cross. Greater love hath no man than this, that a man lay down his life for his friends, that is the love of the Crucified. Only in the cross of Christ do we find the fulfillment of the law."

"We must learn to live in the skin of another man, so we can feel the nailprints in his palms." (Morris West)

Are you willing to say to our black brothers and sisters — and all others who have suffered such massive injustice: "I will be glad to spend all I have, and myself as well, in order to help you"? (2 Corinthians 12:15)

We've only just begun . . .

No paternalism, tokenism, or masochism on our part . . .

We've got a long way to go . . .

How Do You Listen?

READ PSALM 69

What's around today? "Credence Clearwater Revival"? "Jefferson Airplane"? "Iron Butterfly"? "Three Dog Night"? "The Rolling Stones"? "Chicago"? "Who"?

The popularity of the groups, the individual singers, the tunes — everything changes so fast that even a magazine article about a musical group is often dated before it appears in print.

As this is written, more songs of *affirmation* are hitting the air waves. Deeply religious (not necessarily Christian) themes come through in many of the scores. And the mood may change tomorrow. So our comments can only be a response to one aspect of the vast field of pop music.

How do you respond to the tunes of the day?

No doubt the response of many an ear-split parent is: "Sheer noise! I can't even *hear,* much less *understand,* the words!" And many songs indeed are more Watusi than they are wordy. Others, however, even if a listener may not be able to understand the words, may communicate a specific mood or a powerful emotion: loneliness, despair, joy, or affirmation of life.

And then other songs, if one can get a copy of the text, may be composed by very skillful writers who say a great deal about life and its values. Political, social, or other polemical themes may come through powerfully — or at times subtly, as witness the drug motif in many tunes: "Love Special Delivery," "Lucy in the Sky with Diamonds," "Yellow Submarine," "The Trip," "Eight Miles High," "Puff the Magic Dragon" (!?)

What songs do you like best? Some of my favorites have been those by Simon and Garfunkel. Take the powerful commentary in "Sounds of Silence" on the failure of communication between people in our day: "People talking without speaking . . . people hearing without listening . . . silence like a cancer grows . . . hear my words that I might reach you . . . take my arm that I might reach you . . . ."

Or note the chilling rejection in "A Most Peculiar Man": "He lived all alone . . . within himself . . . he turned on the gas and he went to sleep . . . what a shame that he's dead, but wasn't he a most peculiar man . . . ."

The message comes through poignantly: the need to break out of our shells and really communicate with one another, to truly love, to accept, to risk hurt that we might help our fellowman.

But in spite of positive elements like these in many songs, other aspects of some tunes may not always be so helpful to listeners. Indeed, Simon and Garfunkel comment on their conception of their task as tunesmiths by saying: "We're not trying to change anything, but pop music has become a prime medium for making some comment about the world for a large audience."

"Not trying to change anything"? Maybe a

commentary on the situation isn't enough. Indeed, it may lead less to "communicating" than to an isolated "communing" with oneself. Or, worse yet, the end result of listening to some of this music may be similar to a viewing of one of Tennessee William's plays. As Robert Elliot Fitch put it: The plays don't so much help man understand his situation so he can do something about it, as they intensify his egotism, his self-pity, and his wallowing in his own masochistic despair!

For look at the one word (in its several forms) that comes through again and again in many of these tunes: "I," "my," "mine"! "I Gotta Be Me!" "I Did It My Way!" In "Sounds of Silence" the pronoun is used 15 times; in "I am a Rock," 29 times.

This calls to mind the classic words of Jean Baptiste Clemence in Albert Camus' *The Fall*: "I am not hard-hearted, far from it—full of pity on the contrary, and with a ready tear to boot. Only, my emotional impulses always turn toward me, my feelings of pity concern *me*. It is not true, after all, that I never loved. I conceived at least one great love in my life, of which *I* was always the object."

To be sure, there is a valid place for the "I" in our Christian lives. Our blessed Lord said: "Love thy neighbor as thyself." We are sinners, and we confess that to God and He forgives through His Son. But we are not to despise ourselves, not to hate ourselves. For we are worth much in God's eyes! He loves us. He accepts us. He gave Himself for us.

But in the other sense, the "I" is not to be worshiped. And that is man's problem today, as it always has been. Luther had a word for it 450 years ago: *curvatus in se:* man "curved in on himself." Yes, man today is not so much "in search of himself" as he is "in love with himself."

And so Simon and Garfunkel may sing: "I am a rock . . . I am an island." But as John Donne put it several centuries ago: "*No* man is an island!"

We *need* each other. We need help from *outside* ourselves. And thank God there is that One who came to rescue us from ourselves *for* a life of service to Him and to our fellowman.

The litany "For Pastor and People" prepared by Pastor Richard Brewer of Faith Lutheran Church, Pleasant Hill, Calif., sums it up very well. He prepared it as a response to Peggy Lee's hit record: "Is That All There Is?"

PASTOR	PEOPLE
Sometimes, Lord, we wonder:	Is that all there is?
Life ebbs away, dull, gray,	each day the same.
Excitement in something new,	something different,
Something with a challenge,	something simply thrilling.
Just doesn't seem to last—	soon becomes nothing at all.
Sometimes, Lord, we wonder:	is that all there is?
And we feel sad, lonely;	life seems empty, without meaning.
No one gets out alive.	nothing makes any difference.
You, Lord, You make the difference!	You came, Jesus, with life and hope!
Your life was full and exciting!	You helped, healed, loved, and taught.
Your death, Jesus,	swallowed up death.
You walked out of the grave	and made all graves temporary!
You enriched life itself	and filled it with joy!
Come, Lord Jesus!	come, fill our lives!
And give us blessings!	important, wonderful gifts!
Forgiveness,	Peace,
Understanding,	Hope,

Healing,	Life,
Compassion,	Love,
Fellowship,	Joy!

We Christians do confess	with faith and insight,
The Spirit making clear,	the Word filling our ears.
You are all there is, Jesus,	You are all there is!
Help us to avoid the sand;	help us build on rock.
Be with us every day	and forever.
With all Your saints	we praise and bless You,
Now and forever! Amen!	Now and forever! Amen!

Some time ago a Menlo Park, Calif., homemaker who had heard of my criticism of the "Philosophy of the I" in many current songs wrote me a postcard, saying, "I really like Simon and Garfunkel, too. But how about 'Bridge Over Troubled Water'?"

At the same time a Bay Area pastor taking my course on "Reaching the Educated Adult" at the Graduate Theological Union in Berkeley shared with me an interpretation of the song by a seventh grader in his parish: "The piano music at the beginning sets a very sad tone. The person addressed in the song is tired, has a poor self-image, lacks friends, is poor, has no place to call home. This man is isolated from everyone and everything. But there is a glimmer of the Gospel each time the refrain is repeated. Then comes the interlude in the song, and the whole symphony comes in and the mood changes . . . the man has experienced the new life in Christ and is living a victorious life . . . he has a friend he can count on."

Ralph J. Gleason in the *San Francisco Chronicle* even spoke of the song as "almost gospel and given a definitely churchy sound in the recording."

How does the Christian react to all this?

An obvious note of caution is in order, namely, that we not "marshal contemporary artists as witnesses to a God whom they do not yet acknowledge" (*Christianity and Crisis,* April 14, 1958). Nor should we see Christ figures in practically any song or movie where a character displays a touch of altruism or self-sacrifice. (Cf. "The Gospel According to Salinger? — On the Detection of Christ-Figures," by Louise Griffin, *Lutheran Forum,* February, 1968.)

Remember how many people tried to do this with *The Graduate?* ("Jesus loves you, Mrs. Robinson, more than you will ever know. . . .") But Simon and Garfunkel say: "The lyrics weren't completed for the film, but they're addressed to women in their 40's, confused by the world of today. The Joe DiMaggio bit refers to the loss of the folk hero. The information asked of Mrs. Robinson 'for the files' refers to the modern inquisition — the computer."

So where are we?

Alan Paton and Liston Pope offer us a challenging thought: "The modern world has such a nostalgia for innocence and compassion, which virtues it believes itself to have lost, that it confuses them with the Divine Nature." * And they go on to ask the compelling question as to *whether a supposed symbol of Christ is actually a Christ-*

* Quoted in "The Christ-Figure in Contemporary Literature," by Donald L. Deffner, in *Concordia Theological Monthly,* May 1963.

figure or just a Christ-hungry individual. Only a Christ-hungry world would be capable of confusing them.

Think about it!

The Guy with the White Hat

READ JAMES 4

Over the years some theologians have noted—and not completely facetiously—a "theological" motif in the adult western. The story goes something like this:

There's this family in the East, see, and they don't like the life of the organization man. They want to break out of the "pattern," out of group-think, out of living in a world which is almost already Orwell's *1984*.

And so they sell their place and they go out west, where they can really be rugged, individualistic Americans. They settle down. Where? Why in Montana, of course, the "Big Sky" country. All is well, until it's discovered that there's a gold mine on their property.

Then the trouble begins. The bad guys, the forces of evil, begin to harrass these people. And these people don't want to take the law into their own hands, but the established church—I mean the sheriff and deputy sheriff in town—aren't giving these people any help.

So these people finally decide to take the law into their own hands. They arm themselves with guns, they arm their children with guns, they arm the cowhands with guns—everybody on the ranch is armed with guns.

At this precise moment, who should come into the drama but a strange, handsome, mystical figure riding on a white horse and with a white hat—dressed all in white. He's masked. And the people are very suspicious of him. So they ask him for a sign. He gives them a silver bullet.

He has a minority figure with him—Tonto.

And the story progresses, until we see the white-clad figure with his friend all tied up in a cave, deep in the bowels of the earth. There is the dynamite keg in the corner, the fuse sputtering away, coming closer and closer . . . .

Suddenly there's a breaking of the bonds. They come out of the cave. They make their way through the woods until they find the bad guys sitting around the campfire, slugging down a couple hookers of liquor.

They get the drop on them. The people get back their ranch—and their gold mine. Good has conquered evil once again! And as the music of Rossini gradually comes up in the background, the people all swell themselves up and recite their creed:

"I believe in Law and Order, maker of peace and happiness.

"And in the Lone Ranger, its truest exponent, conceived in nobility, born of Mystery, was shunned by society in general, beaten by robbers, buried in apparent death.

"But three seconds later he arose again to prominence, and lives and fights as the right hand of Law and Order.

"And I believe in faithful Tonto. I belong to the fan clubs, sharing TV and box-tops; I wish life could be like that for me, from one week to the next.*
* *"HI-YO!"* ("Creed" by William A. Kaeppel)

How aware are we of the subtle forces and philosophies which can impinge on us through the mass media and which can give us a warm, emotional, almost liturgical "bath" on a Saturday night before the boob tube—and which can provide a handy substitute for the fellowship of the church and need for the Lord's Table on a Sunday morning?

In *The Electronic Gospel* William Kuhns has even suggested an apparent liturgy in "Mission: Impossible." There is the lit fuse going across the bottom of the screen, and the montage of shots as the theme for the week—that's the introit.

Then there is "The Plan." You hear a tape or record of the voice: "Your mission, Jim, should you decide to accept it . . . ." That's the Epistle and Gospel for the day.

Then comes "The Plan Enacted." That's the sermon.

And finally there are the credits and the windup—the offering, prayers, and benediction!

One analyst even saw a catchy religious hook for the Christian audience in terms of a baptismal drowning and resurrection motif in a Volkswagen ad where a priest's almost-human beetle floated him to safety out of an icy North Dakota lake!

To what extent do you watch television critically? How often do you muse as you view a program: "*Is* that the meaning and purpose of life?" How carefully do you catch the philosophies of life which may be implied: "That's the way things are," "Everybody's doing it," "I can't help myself," "Whatever will be, will be," etc.?

We need to be ever more aware of the false world views and "gods of the land" (Deuteronomy 6:14) around us which can become subtle substitutes for Him who said: "Thou shalt worship the Lord thy God, and Him only shalt thou serve." (Matthew 4:10 KJV)

And Paul's words come to mind once more: "Don't let the world around you squeeze you into its own mould. But let God re-mould your minds from within, so that you may prove in practice that the Plan of God for you is good, meets all His demands and moves towards the goal of true maturity." (Romans 12: 2 Phillips)

Celebrating His Presence

Many people in the church used to think of the task of the church as "following its college students to the campus." Such phrases were used as "taking Christ to the university." This type of thinking was consonant with the idea that the college or university was somehow antichristian or unchristian by its very nature; and this further gave rise to many anti-intellectual, anti-higher-education, and obscurantist views in the church.

Happily, in recent years many in the church have realized how erroneous this kind of thinking was. We now realize that Christ is on campus; in fact, He has been there all the time.

First of all, Christ is on campus because all the academic disciplines and subjects which treat the nature of the world and man in it are actually concerned with *God's* world—it is His creation. And bit by bit whatever research is conducted and whatever discoveries are made are "breakthroughs" that God is permitting man to make as he plumbs deeper and deeper into the mysteries and wonders of God's vast created cosmogony. One might well ask, What has God been doing in the sciences these days?

Further, Christ is on campus, for He walks to and fro every day on the campus paths and up and down the halls of the classroom buildings, in the hearts and lives of the Christ-men and

Christ-women who bear His name. They are His witnesses. And wherever they go, Christ goes and makes His call and challenge and claim on other students who still do not know Him.

Among non-Christian students the sentiment is often found that truth is somehow "on campus," in the empirical and scientific approach to subject matter. The student chapels and student centers are off-campus, are viewed as doctrinaire, and whatever good they may produce is substandard to the "truth" which is found in the high halls of learning.

The concept, of course, is erroneous; it is a dogmatism all of its own making. But there is a grain of truth in the idea too—for truth *is* on campus, because whatever is discovered is God's truth already. He is the Author and the Finisher of everything. "For in Him all things were created, in heaven and on earth, visible and invisible, whether thrones or dominions or principalities or authorities—all things were created through Him and for Him. He is before all things, and in Him all things hold together." (Colossians 1:16-17)

So let us celebrate His presence on campus!

Not Ashamed

READ ROMANS 1

Several students were walking across the quadrangle of a large university just as the bell tower chimed five o'clock in the afternoon. At that precise moment in front of them on the sidewalk a foreign student dropped full length on the ground to the utter amazement of those walking behind him. After the initial shock the students realized that he had not stumbled or fallen but was a Moslem who was prostrating himself at his holy hour of prayer.

That man was not ashamed of his religion. How many of us are not ashamed to make known that we are Christians: through prayer before meals in the campus cafeteria, before studying in the library, or upon beginning that heavy examination in the classroom?

How many of us by omission of prayer, or other practices that might designate that we are Christians, in effect become guilty of the sin of the apostle Peter when he said: "I do not know the Man"? (Matthew 26:74)

What a tragedy for those who have been nominal members of the church, but about whom Christ will one day say: "And then will I declare to them, 'I never knew you'"! (Matthew 7:23)

The positive challenge of Scripture is: "Let your light so shine before men that they may see your good works and give glory to your Father who is in heaven" (Matthew 5:16). We are to be

63

"innocent and pure, as God's perfect children who live in a world of crooked and mean people." (Philippians 2:15 TEV)

"If a man is ashamed of Me and of My teaching, then the Son of Man will be ashamed of him when He comes in His glory and the glory of the Father and of the holy angels. Remember this! There are some here . . . who will not die until they have seen the kingdom of God." (Luke 9:26-27)

Therefore let us say with the apostle Paul: "I am not ashamed of the Gospel; it is the power of God for salvation to everyone who has faith." (Romans 1:16)

"Pastor, She's Gone"

READ PSALM 104

It had been a long vigil during those last few months. The campus pastor and his parishioner had sat by the bedside of the young man's wife. She had terminal cancer. But the time finally came when the phone rang at the parsonage a little after midnight, and he heard the words at the other end of the line: "Pastor, she's gone."

All the resources of medical research had been drained to try to save this young woman's life, but to no avail — another life was over. Help for this young woman, both human and technological, stopped at death's door.

God has permitted man to discover many things in the various sciences. And the Christian student sees all research and the use of the scientific method as God's own gift to him. But at the same time he recognizes the limitations, the definitive limitations of these tools. Even if and when scientists synthetically "create" life, the question will still remain as to the Author behind "life," matter, and energy in the first place.

Note how the whole of Scripture and the whole of life is stamped with those mighty first four words of the Book of Genesis: "In the beginning God." "From Him and through Him and to Him are all things" (Romans 11:36). And ultimately beyond all that God has permitted us to discover about man and the world in which he lives, it is our majestic Creator-God with whom we have to deal.

Truly, "He did not leave Himself without witness" (Acts 14:17). But God's majesty is evident not only in all the wonders of this creation but also in coming to us in the form of His beloved Son. It is in Him that we find the purpose of all the universes — and of our own lives.

His Own Mental Construct

READ PSALM 33

James A. Pike edited the book *Modern Canterbury Pilgrims,* which consists of a number of essays by prominent men who describe why they chose the Episcopal Church. One of them, John H. Hallowell, tells how he was first attracted to Christianity once he was shown that it was intellectually relevant to the problems with which he was professionally concerned.

But long before this in the course of his academic career other men had had a profoundly negative influence on him in contributing to the demolition of whatever Christian faith he had as a youth. He recalls one man: "But my genial professor, a true skeptic to the last, closed the course as he began it, with a quizzical smile, and while I came away admiring his dialectical skill, I also came away with a sense of the intellectual futility of seeking answers to the most basic questions."

Professors on secular college campuses are not, categorically, "atheistic ogres who try to destroy the faith of gullible freshmen." But it is always good to keep in mind the question: Is the professor at this point dealing solely with the facts of the case, or is he now putting his own mental construct on things? Is he being true to his own discipline, or has he stepped out of his field to make comments on his own?

Even as in doctrinal and spiritual matters

the Christian student does not believe every spirit but tests the spirits "to see whether they are of God" (1 John 4:1), so in the academic world he will listen critically to whatever presentations are made. He will be aware of the purely "human point of view" that can enter into his professor's statements; but he will also welcome the testing and the challenge which the professor's confrontation provides him.

Lasting Drama

READ LUKE 15

Did you ever think of the Holy Communion service as a drama? It is—high drama.

In fact, this play with its characters, its gripping plot, and theme has been playing to packed houses for 20 centuries. The story is almost melodramatic. It is the story of a lost child, a child who has rejected everything that his father has done for him. But it is also a story of *rapprochement,* of reconciliation between the erring child and the loving, forgiving father.

It is, of course, the drama of salvation—of man's salvation. The one place where the analogy does not hold is in that we were not spectators to this great reenactment of the history of man's relationship with God as it is played out on the stage before us in the chancel. No, we are not observers; we are all a key character—the erring prodigal who has run away from the family of God.

Isaiah's words apply to us: "Your iniquities have made a separation between you and your God, and your sins have hid His face from you so that He does not hear" (Isaiah 59:2). So we must say with David: "Against Thee, Thee only have I sinned and done that which is evil in Thy sight." (Psalm 51:4)

Then we will also share in the end of the drama. It is the story told in so many beautiful ways in Luke 15: The one lost sheep is found by the shepherd, and he rejoices; the one lost coin is found after a diligent search, and the woman rejoices with her neighbors; and the prodigal son returns to the waiting father, who says: "We'll have to have a celebration. I thought my son was dead, and he is alive; I thought he was lost, and he is found!"

Let's say it again: "What a wonderful God we have!"

By the Skin of Your Teeth

READ ROMANS 3

Students at some universities turn in self-addressed postcards with their final examination papers; thus they need not wait long to learn what their final grades are. One fellow always glued four-leaf clovers to his cards, with the comment, "Usually it helps."

I remember seeing one student's postcard after it had been returned; on it the reader had scribbled in red pencil, "A — by the skin of your teeth."

Some people would like to get to heaven if only "by the skin of their teeth." But there is some horribly warped thinking in this conception of Christianity.

For one thing, in the final analysis one doesn't "get to heaven" by anything that he does. It is totally God at work in him. And this is what many people have difficulty seeing. From outside the context of faith, "believing on the Lord Jesus Christ" looks like the deliberate choice of man's own will.

But once he has stepped through the doorway of faith, the Christian realizes the step, the very desire to return to Christ, was the blessed action of the Holy Spirit. (Nor was it against the Christian's will to resist.) And looking up through the spectacles of faith he now sees and comprehends the sign over the inside of the door: "The only way you got in here was by the grace of God."

In that sense, and in that sense alone, are we

saved "by the skin of our teeth." Without the grace of God, without the crowning resurrection miracle which proves that we shall one day be raised from the dead, our faith is vain; we are "still in our sins" (1 Corinthians 15:17). But Christ did rise from the dead, our faith is not futile, and we have the certainty of lively life in God now and into all eternity.

Salvage Operation

READ 2 TIMOTHY 3

"Students don't lose their faith in college! If this is said, they didn't have any faith when they got there."

There is a lot of truth in these statements. Even Philip E. Jacobs' famous study *Changing Values in College* bears out the fact that students do not essentially change their value structure during their academic years. The point is that the values, the beliefs, the attitudes about life have usually crystallized several years before one comes to the halls of ivy.

To this extent some of the church's work is a "salvage operation" – seeking to repair damage that has been done or seeking to implement and improve training in Christian truth that a student may never have properly or fully received. (This is not to exclude the crucial thrust of our campus ministry as *mission*.)

Look back in your own life. What kind of spiritual development did you have during the four years before you came to college? Did you read Scripture regularly, commune faithfully and penitently, live with the rich fellowship of other Christians, and grow in your knowledge of Scripture? In many cases a Christian student may still be maintaining a conception of a "little God" which has hardly kept up with his growth in other areas of knowledge.

Why not "be scientific" about it? Why not take

a good look at your Christian faith again and see if it has the maturity, the depth, and the contemporaneity it should?

This will mean study of the Scriptures; it will mean discussion with other Christians; it will mean counsel with a campus pastor – a thorough and systematic investigation of Christian doctrine.

A woman who is a professor of English literature at a girls' college once invited me to speak to several of her classes on "Theology and Contemporary Literature." I made the point that even as we do not "read into" Hemingway a view that is not really his own in the book, so we should come to the Scriptures with an open mind and let it speak to us from within itself. The woman was amazed at the insight – a principle which she actually had been trying to get across to her students all year long as they studied various works of literature. She said, "You know, I think I'm going to go back and read the Bible all over again, keeping in mind that principle that you suggested."

Try it! Just how mature is your faith?

It can be a challenging and exhilarating adventure as you discover all over again the depth, the height, the length, and the breadth of the Christian faith in your own life and a God who is more contemporary than you have ever realized He could be. And you too can be amazed at what the grace and gift of God in Christ can do in you as God rebuilds your faith.

Foul Balls in the Pew

READ ACTS 2

"Don't tell me what you are because what you do speaks so loudly." We usually judge a person by what he does, not just by what he says. "Deeds, not creeds!"

Many people outside the church have refused to step into its fellowship because of the inconsistencies and contradictions which they have noted in the lives of those who claim to be "good Christians." And yet the church — like any group within society — has its share of "foul balls." Man, not being a puppet, has freedom to act at great variance from what he should be.

Although the hypocrites and weak Christians who are obvious to outsiders are a stumbling block to others in becoming members of Christ's fellowship, the ultimate question still remains: What are you doing with Christ and His claim on your life? In the final analysis, all the false "Christians" in the world cannot be an excuse for a person's not coming to terms with this great God-man standing at history's turning point.

A Christian is really a signpost pointing to Christ. He says, "Don't just look at me and my life. I may be a poor witness at times to the Christian faith, but I am striving every day by God's grace to do better. Look at Him who has given me forgiveness for my sins and constantly gives me power to be a better self. You belong to this Christ. What are you doing with Him?"

READ MATTHEW 23

In his incisive novel *The Fall* Albert Camus gives a penetrating description of a retired Parisian lawyer. The protagonist, John Baptiste Clemence, is obsessed by an overwhelming self-love and by a constant drive to dominate and use and manipulate other people. He speaks of "keeping them in the refrigerator" so that he can bring them out whenever he wants to make use of them for his own ends and purposes.

This is a besetting problem for all of us— Christians who are still plagued by the presence of the old Adam in our hearts. We are so often prone to use other people as means rather than as ends. We like to manipulate them to serve our own purposes and desires rather than to see these people as ends in themselves to be served and helped and loved. To dominate and manipulate other people, to see them only as tools by which we get what we want, is really a horrible thing. In one sense it is a form of prostitution and destroys the worth that God has placed into every human being. Christ came not to be served but to serve. It is our calling to determine how we can help others, not just "use them" to help us get what we want.

Look around. Who is there that you have been climbing over and using as a tool to get to the top of some goal that you have set for yourself?

"Nor should you be called 'Leader,' because

your one and only Leader is the Messiah. The greatest one among you must be your servant." (Matthew 23:10-11 TEV) "It was to this that God called you; because Christ Himself suffered for you and left you an example, so that you would follow in His steps." (1 Peter 2:21 TEV)

"I Can't Stand Her!"

READ 1 CORINTHIANS 12

"Pastor, I know that you're not supposed to hate anybody," she began. "But is it alright if you just can't stand someone?"

Will Rogers once said, "I never met a man I didn't like." Not all of us could say that as we look back upon every person we have known during our lives, especially on campus, where the pressures and exigencies of the academic routine often bring very different personalities into conflict. The apostle Paul speaks of the "difference of gifts" we all have. What uniqueness God has given each of us! There is no one else in the world exactly like you!

But although we may have radically different personalities, characters, and life-styles, the joy of our being together is that we can still have "the same spirit." And the same pardon from our Lord! As David Owren says, "We are not all the same, except in God's forgiveness."

In 1 Corinthians 12 Paul tells how much we all need one another, how we suffer with one another, how we share in one another's joys and sorrows. We are "one in spirit," for by the Holy Spirit we have been made one in Christ, the Head.

You can be "different" in the church, for it is a difference God has given. But you are bound into a unity with all other Christians by the Christ who makes it possible to find completeness in the midst of all of our differences.

READ ROMANS 12

Did you ever take a course in which you wondered where in the world the professor was going? There just didn't seem to be any rhyme or reason in his conduct of the course.

I once had such a course in sociology. It was about the driest and dullest thing I had ever sat through. Nevertheless, I faithfully took notes throughout the semester and worked hard just on the principle of the thing, hoping I would ultimately get something out of it. To my utter amazement about six months later I used much of the structure of the course and the principles I had learned in it for a major piece of graduate work.

Houston Peterson in *Great Teachers* notes that when some lecturers finish what they have been talking about, the conclusions are there; they have been neatly measured and packaged, and everybody feels pleased. But nobody cares to come back to the subject again.

In contrast to such teachers he noted those who come to grips with real problems and are not too systematic in their presentation; when they finish their lecture, there are a lot of "loose ends," but they are "live ends," and you can do something with them.

Our Christian lives are often this way too. They are not neatly packaged with all problems solved and all answers given to all the questions that we raise about the whys of life. We are plagued by tensions of many kinds in our campus life—worrying about being accepted by other people, worrying about the term paper or the assignment that is almost due, worrying about whether we will meet expenses for the year.

But above and behind the whole campus scene there is One who knows everything that is going on in our lives. He is not pulling puppet strings but is letting us pass through the tests and trials of life that we might better realize our need and dependency on Him.

We hear someone speak of "God's plan for your life" and decide that it is certainly a non-systematic job so far as our lives are concerned. But God has given us some "live ends" by which we might find the direction for our lives and know that He is still in control of all that lies ahead.

These live ends are the life-giving forgive-ness of sins found in His precious Word, in the renewal of our baptismal vow each day, and in the regular, penitent use of the Lord's Supper. When we have these reins in our hands, we can know right where we are going, even though we can't see the final destination clearly.

J. B. Phillips put it this way in his paraphrase of Romans 12:2: "Let God remould your minds from within, so that you may prove in practice that the plan of God for you is good, meets all His demands, and moves toward the goal of true maturity."

There's a Difference

READ 2 CORINTHIANS 10

James D. Smart in his excellent educational text, *The Teaching Ministry of the Church,* tells of a group of high school teachers who were asked to teach a new curriculum in the youth department of their church. The course was titled "Christ and Humanism." It included noting distinctions between such approaches as Dale Carnegie's *How to Win Friends and Influence People* and the teachings of Christ in the New Testament.

After studying the materials, these teachers refused to teach the course, saying that they saw no valid distinction or contradiction between Christianity and humanism. To them Dale Carnegie and Christ were "just good companions," and Christianity and humanism were "inextricably intermingled."

Here was a tragic case of people who had nominally grown up as Christians, but their approach to life was that of humanism—that "man is the measure of all things."

Is man the measure? Second Corinthians 10 has something to say about this. It speaks of "casting down imaginations and every high thing that exalteth itself against the knowledge of God, and bringing into captivity every thought to the obedience of Christ" (2 Corinthians 10:5 KJV). Paul goes on to say that the only "measure" that man really has is the rule which God has set for

81

us: "As the Scripture says, 'Whoever wants to boast, must boast of what the Lord has done.' Because a man is really approved when the Lord thinks well of him, not when he thinks well of himself." (2 Corinthians 10:17-18 TEV)

Man is not the measure of all things, but God is the Great Measurer. "It is He that made us and not we ourselves." His measure of man reads: "There is not a righteous man on earth who does good and never sins" (Ecclesiastes 7:20). Humanism radically rejects this, saying that man is essentially good and has within himself the power to overcome the problems that face mankind.

But "there is no difference, for all have sinned and come short of the glory of God, being justified freely by His grace through the redemption that is in Christ Jesus" (Romans 3:22-24 KJV). Thank God, there is a measure for all of us who have come short of God's rule—He is the greatest "human" of them all, but also the Son of God and the Savior of the world. In Him alone is our only real hope.

Yes, there is a difference!

Univertere

READ PSALM 89

Some critics of the modern university have accused it of academic schizophrenia and dubbed it the "multiversity." The contemporary seat of learning is no longer the university of the 13th century, where theology was queen and the very etymology of the word was true: *univertere* – to combine together into one.

Rather, today's school has many different departments and disciplines, unrelated to religion and often as quite separate entities unto themselves. One person said that the only thing that connects the various departments on his campus is the plumbing.

As the church looks at the fragmented state of much secular college and university education today, it engages in dialog with the university so that both churchman and educator may together take into account the whole man who is being educated. Church and university – each has a unique function. The secular university does not exist to give the collegian one specific *Weltanschauung* or religious faith. But it should posit the need for a philosophy of life, for an integrating principle for the multiplicity of courses and studies which the student undertakes. Church and university are therefore partners in the educational enterprise. And the student benefits from the resources of each, the rational and the spiritual, the natural and the eternal.

Church and university—they are both gifts of God to man. And for the benefits which come from each the renewed Christian praises and thanks God, "from whom all blessings flow."

A Mission to Us

READ HEBREWS 11

A certain exchange student had been a Christian for only a few years. After a brief period of study and visiting in the United States she and her husband returned to her homeland. Not long afterward her husband died suddenly.

In writing to a friend in America, commenting on the death, this fledgling Christian puzzled over why God had let him die, but the letter carried no bitterness or complaint. Instead she wrote: "Christ never, never leave me down. My eyes are full of tears with happiness, remembering *small* treasures. I'll never stop singing songs to praise my Christ Child. Lord makes me brave. I take Bible everywhere and do not hesitate to sing and pray among non-Christian friends. I cannot die, because Christ insists me to live and to work for His glory. I am His slave."

What a testimony of faith! We often speak of having a "mission" to people in foreign lands. But when one looks at the apathy in many of our churches, in the lives of many of our people, and then hears a testimony of faith like this, one is tempted to say that these young Christians and young churches in other lands have a mission to *us*. Maybe they can bring us back to the original fire and burning enthusiasm of faith which it so often seems we have lost.

Let us pray with the hymn writer:

Send Thou, O Lord, to every place
Swift messengers before Thy face,
The heralds of Thy wondrous grace,
Where Thou Thyself wilt come.
Send men whose eyes have seen the King,
Men in whose ears His sweet words ring . . .

Walking on the Moon

READ COLOSSIANS 3

John Dewey used to say that the only thing that we can be certain of is change itself.

Many things certainly have changed in the world's history. Man's conception of his universe has changed from his being awed with the earth on which he walked to looking at the universe of planets around him to finally realizing that it was not a universe but rather millions of universes extending far beyond the mind's comprehension. And now we "walk on the moon and make a mess on the earth." (George G. Parker)

There has also been much change in terms of man's attempts to live in the strange, new world which has been foisted upon him; and many writers have spoken of the different kinds of "man" which are needed to fill the gap between where we are now and where various explorations will take us in the future.

We quite often forget, however, to examine the facets of the "new man" of whom the New Testament speaks and who the Christian church holds is the only answer to meet the problems of this new age.

This is the new man we become through faith in our Lord and Savior Jesus Christ. He is at once God's revelation to us of the persons we are to be, and the transforming power to become such new individuals. It is true, our cosmology has changed, our culture has shifted, our verbal symbols and media of communication have been transposed. But sinful men are still the same today, and our God is still the same. The truth still remains, the challenge to each one of us: "Put on the new man, which after God is created in righteousness and true holiness" (Ephesians 4:23 KJV). Only then is man—the Christian man—prepared to live in a strange, new world.

Forgotten You're Forgiven?

READ PSALM 51

The black-haired co-ed had been sitting in the pastor's study for about an hour, complaining bitterly about the treatment other members in the choir had been giving her. Finally, after a long pause, the girl looked up and said quietly, "But this isn't my real problem, Pastor. My real difficulty is that I have been sleeping with my fiance, and I just had to talk to you about it."

Then the real counseling began. The pastor assured the girl of God's forgiveness if there was true penitence on her part for what she had been doing. He went on to demonstrate the difference between God's forgiveness and forgiveness as many human beings think of it, for they may often say, "Oh, sure, I forgive you, but I don't see how I can forget about it!" This is in sharp contrast to God's forgiveness, which is really a full pardon. A pardon does not mean a crime was never committed but rather that the crime and its debt have been fully accounted for and the record is now wiped clean. This is the blessed gift that is now ours because of the death of Christ on the cross for our sins.

Here are the amazing and heartwarming words of our God Himself in Isaiah 43:25: "I, I am He who blots out your transgressions for My own sake, and I will not remember your sins."

Just think, we have the kind of God who not

only forgives but no longer even remembers our sins.

I believe it was O. P. Kretzmann who once made the comment that we should learn to pray something like this: "O Lord, forgive me for the sin of coming back to you and asking forgiveness for sins which you forgave and forgot a long time ago."

What a God! What a pardon!

"Have you forgotten you're forgiven? Remember the lasting quality of God's forgiveness. Forgiveness is never old. It's always new. As new as sin itself." (David Owren)

The Hound of Heaven

READ ISAIAH 40

She was working on her doctorate in chemistry, the students at the chapel remembered. And they never forgot the time she first visited the student center. She had wandered in and accosted one of the students lounging in the vestibule and said, "I am an atheist. Argue with me." To this the other student replied calmly, "Why, we don't argue with anybody around here. Come on in."

The young woman stayed for three years, even sang in the choir, but did not join the church. Nevertheless, she often admitted the strong pull of the Gospel message, which she somehow couldn't quite accept. At one time she confided to the campus pastor, "I just can't see believing in all that you do. But sometimes I still feel that God is chasing after me. You know, Pastor Don, the hound of heaven may get me yet."

She, of course, was referring to the famous poem by Francis Thompson, "The Hound of Heaven." For years the author himself had tried hard to escape from God. He had turned to many poor substitutes, but all in vain:

I fled Him down the nights and down the days;
I fled Him down the arches of the years;
I fled Him down the labyrinthine ways
Of my own mind; and in the mist of tears
I hid from Him, and under running laughter.
Up vistaed hopes I sped;

And shot, precipitated,
Adown titanic glooms of charmed fears,
From those strong feet that followed,
    followed after.

This is the true picture of our God, a brooding, loving, concerned God, who all down through history chased after those who ran away from Him, yes, also after you and me in so many ways in our daily lives.

Even we who have been in the church for many years can still be "hiding from God." And we need to come face to face with our Creator and honestly and open-mindedly examine the claims He makes on our lives.

We need to learn to say over and over again: "Lord, what wilt Thou have me to do?" We need to listen to the loving and concerned call of our Savior and Redeemer, the One who in His infinite love suffered and died and rose again.

He is the One who says: "Behold, I stand at the door and knock. If anyone hears My voice and opens the door, I will come in to him and eat with him, and he with Me." (Revelation 3:20)

Quo vadis?

READ GALATIANS 1

What are you doing with your life? What vocation have you chosen? Every Christian student might well consider whether God wants him to go into "professional" church work. (The term "professional" is used rather than "full-time" because every person is a "full-time" Christian.) Scrutiny should be given not only to the preaching or teaching ministry but to many other phases of missionary work, social welfare under the auspices of the church, the work of a deaconess, youth ministry, and others.

Now God may well want you to be the very best engineer, nurse, teacher, economist that you can be; and this is just as noble a calling in His eyes as is professional church service. But some students have not seriously considered such church work because they feel personally unworthy of what in their minds is so high and holy a calling.

But those in the church who have taken up this specialized service hardly feel "worthy" themselves. Nor did they have an "ecstatic experience" in most cases but rather a growing conviction that this was what God wanted them to do with their lives. They learned to depend on Him for His promise of grace, His gift of faith, His power. They knew it was "not because of any good works that we ourselves had done, but because of His own mercy" (Titus 3:5 TEV) that it was possible for them to enter this specialized work.

Faith and spirituality are not qualities that we "trump up" within ourselves. The Holy Spirit alone is the One who gives us the new life and the ability to serve Him. He does that in us which we are utterly unable to do.

Peanuts

In one "Peanuts" comic strip one of the female small fry came to Charlie Brown and said, "Yes, sir, Charlie Brown, Abraham Lincoln was a great man. Charlie Brown, would you like to have been Abraham Lincoln?"

"Well, now, I don't think so," he replied slowly; "I am having a hard enough time being just plain old Charlie Brown."

We often have a hard time learning to accept ourselves as we are. This does not mean that we are not to improve our Christian character with God's help and make the most of such gifts as we have. But we often bring a great deal of anxiety upon ourselves because we are trying to be a person whom we can't become.

We may admire another individual whose talents far outweigh our own, and we feel terribly guilty and inferior as we compare ourselves with that individual. Or we may actually compensate by "cutting that person down to size" through malicious gossip or some other way of "giving him a bad time."

But this anxiety is needless. Scripture says: "I bid everyone among you not to think of himself more highly than he ought to think but to think with sober judgment" (Romans 12:3 KJV). This calls for real humility. It involves an appreciation and full use of the talents, gifts, and abilities that God has given one, balanced on the

95

other hand by a recognition of the limits of personality potential with which one is endowed.

God does not expect me to be a person other than myself. But he does expect me to make a full use of my God-given abilities and to live a life of integrity and faithfulness before Him. The question is not: How am I doing in comparison to other people? But the question is: How am I doing in comparison with God's will and standard for my life?

"It is required in stewards that a man be found faithful." (1 Corinthians 4:2 KJV)

One Christian put it this way: "When I die I will not be asked, 'Why were you not St. Paul, why were you not Luther, why were you not this or that great leader in the church?' I will be asked, 'Why were you not *you*?' "

Sex Is Here to Stay

READ 1 CORINTHIANS 10

It had been a long and involved and emotional discussion in the student center that Sunday evening on the topic "The Christian Interpretation of Sex." Everyone heaved a sigh as the conversation drew to an end and the moderator asked, "Are there any more questions or additional comments to be made?"

To this one thin voice replied from the rear of the room, "Well, I think sex is here to stay."

Yes, sex is here to stay. Indeed, God meant it to be that way. So often we may get the idea, somehow, that sex is intrinsically bad or dirty or that it is somehow involved only with the body — and the body somehow corrupts the rest of one's being.

Ed Wessling once delivered an insightful sermon on "The Christian Interpretation of Sex." In it he notes how Scripture speaks of man as a unity. And God made this unity. Indeed God made sex. So He must be in favor of it. And this is one of the first clues towards our understanding of this gift of God. God wants you to be the very best male or female that you possibly can be. He created you with your sexuality.

Second, sex has not only to do with the physical — our body — but it is a total union of two people emotionally, spiritually, and from it can come a communion of two personalities which is one of the most beautiful gifts which God has given to man. This total oneness, of course, can be destroyed if one views sex as the only purpose of marriage or for that matter as the primary relationship between a young man and a young woman in dating or courtship. Here, most subtly, if sex is viewed only as a means to an end, two people can become things; human worth and integrity are destroyed, and the real unity of two personalities which could be built up is left in shambles.

The true meaning of sex, then, is understood only in the light of two people as they see their friendship, their courtship, or their marriage under the perspective of God's presence and God's promises. In the self-giving of Christ on the cross we see the clue towards a proper use of our own sexuality — in denying oneself for the other person and making full use of our sexual powers only within that blessed estate of marriage where God has said He would bless.

Let no one say that God leaves the Christian young man or woman without help in these days of a sex-saturated culture. God has a promise that really works in this case; it is 1 Corinthians 10:12-13: "Therefore let anyone who thinks that he stands take heed lest he fall. No temptation has overtaken you that is not common to man. God is faithful, and He will not let you be tempted beyond your strength but with the temptation will also provide the way of escape that you may be able to endure it."

This is a tremendous promise, isn't it? When temptations to impurity come one's way, God has promised that there is a way of escape if we will but look for it.

It may mean turning immediately to prayer for God's help in time of testing. It may mean learning how to sublimate and throw ourselves into other activities. It may mean getting the help of a friend who will be able to give us the Christian guidance and counsel that we need. It may mean simply learning how to run away from the temptation by using those gifts of our two legs.

Most certainly Scripture is always by our side, and we can turn to it for grace to help in time of need. Indeed the Word of God comes to us again and again with God's promises of help. "Call upon Me in the day of trouble; I will deliver you, and you shall glorify Me." (Psalm 50:15)

A final escape hatch may be one of the most difficult of all to use — simply learning how to say no! But God Himself will give each individual the strength to say no when that individual is immersed in God's holy Word and is using the sacraments penitently and regularly.

So there you are; there are the "ways of escape for you" which God has promised to have available in your hour of temptation.

Sex is here to stay. Indeed God gave you your sexuality. He will also give you the grace to use it as a blessing. He will enable you to praise Him and serve your future life partner through your sexuality.

Cheering in Church?

READ PSALM 99

In his *Plain Christianity* J. B. Phillips tells the story of an exciting evening at a youth center in London. There had been dancing, speeches and cheers, and singing "For He's a Jolly Good Fellow." At the end of the evening he suggested that the group have some worship.

One person spoke up bluntly, "You know, we haven't any idea what you really mean by worship!"

"Haven't you?" he responded. "Well, it's three cheers for God!"

So often we may come to church to have our problems solved, to get help for spiritual life, to get our mind off our difficulties on campus, or for more mundane reasons like "it simply being Sunday morning" or "having nothing else better to do."

But many of our problems and anxieties would fade away if we could just get our eyes focused back on the goal of our earthly pilgrimage and on our heavenly Father, who knows all the things that we really need.

What we must do is "lose ourselves" in worship and adoration and praise of this great God of ours. *Adoramus te, Christe!* "We adore Thee, O Christ!" This should be our theme song as we extol the wonder and greatness of our loving, beneficent God.

Think of the high points that come in the

service, for example, during the Sanctus in the Holy Communion service. The semicircle of communicants standing in the chancel is completed on the other end by a semicircle of angels around the throne of God also chanting in unison: "Holy, holy, holy, Lord God of Sabaoth!"

If we can catch this vision of angels round the throne worshiping and glorifying God — our own task into all eternity — then we are on the road towards the spirit of true worship.

Look at your life this day. This time don't look at the burdens but at the blessings which are yours. Consider such gifts as those that God has given you. Above all, remember that He has given His own blessed Son into death for your sins.

If one has caught the height and depth and breadth and length of God's love for us, how could he help but sing, "Three cheers for God!"

Is Love the Key?

READ 1 JOHN 4

It was a morning convocation during Religious Emphasis Week at Oklahoma State University in Stillwater. The guest speaker had just finished, and the crowd was heading for the doors. A number of students came down to the rostrum. Among them was a Moslem student, who said to the speaker, "I enjoyed your talk very much, but I cannot agree with you as to the exclusiveness of Christianity and your implication that believing in Christ is the only true religion. I believe that the one great theme of all religions is love. Don't you? If a man has love — whether he is a Jew, a Moslem, a Christian, or whatever — isn't that the only important thing?"

Love certainly is the greatest thing that is needed in the affairs of men and nations in this tumultuous age of ours. But a man may "love" and still live a life which ignores God, who is the Author of all love. This is the tragedy of many a life — the "good agnostic," the well-meaning humanist, the altruist in the helping professions, the "good guy" on campus, who may be very selfless in many of the things that he or she does but has never really given God the glory for "the good" which is being done.

Someone has said, "These people are drinking from a stream, the source of which they deny." Again the questions must be raised: Who made you? Where did you come from? What is the

102

origin and source of this power of love and forgiveness which you grant is so needed in the affairs of men and nations?

Christ said: "He who abides in Me, and I in him, he it is that bears much fruit, for apart from Me you can do nothing" (John 15:5). In Hebrews we read: "Without faith it is impossible to please Him" (Hebrews 11:6). And so, much as we respect the "civil righteousness" of men, it is not "good" in God's eyes. Only when God in Christ is acknowledged as the Author and Source of this love is man doing "the good" from an eternal perspective.

For the fountain and wellspring of love was opened up on Calvary that Good Friday when a spear pierced Christ's side, and blood and water flowed forth. It was in Christ's death that the greatest love of all was shown in His giving Himself into the pangs of hell for all of us. From that fountain flows the life-giving forgiveness of sins in the water of Holy Baptism and the body and blood of Holy Communion.

"In this is love, not that we loved God but that He loved us and sent His Son to be the expiation for our sins." (1 John 4:10)

Not Really Concerned

READ JOHN 4

A Christian student once told me that in his life in a dormitory he had been trying to reach one particular young man who was not a Christian. They had had a number of conversations over a period of months, but one day his friend said to him: "Look, Lloyd, I'm not nearly as concerned as you think I am."

Sometimes Christians may be a little naive in their understanding of "the children of this world." After years of living without God, after years of no contact with Christian people or the means of grace by which God reveals Himself to man, a person may well be able to say in all sincerity, "I don't know what you're talking about" when a Christian begins to discuss Christian truths with him. There may or may not be true atheists, but there certainly are some sincere skeptics, who say, "I just don't know," and some sincere agnostics, who say, "I cannot know absolute truth."

Some of these people indeed may actually have passed the "point of no return." After a repeated hardening of one's heart, God may give one over to a permanent hardness of the heart, as He did in the case of Pharaoh in the Old Testament or in the case of homosexuals referred to in Romans 1:26-27.

This, of course, does not mean that the Christian student "gives up" in his witness to all people. Nor should he lose heart in his desire to present the Gospel to all with whom he comes in contact.

Remember the day in Christ's ministry when in His own hometown people refused to believe in Him? The Scripture says He could not do any "mighty works" there but only healed a few sick folk. "And He marveled because of their unbelief."

If the Son of God and Son of Man "marveled" at the unbelief of people who had seen God in the flesh, need we despair when we do not see "results" in our witnessing and proclaiming of the Gospel?

Years ago a lady wrote to Walter A. Maier, the Lutheran Hour speaker, saying that she had prayed for her husband's conversion for 35 years but now had practically given up hope. What was she to do? she asked. To this Dr. Maier wrote back, "Keep praying for him. Maybe in the 36th year!"

It is not our task to be "effective," "successful," nor always to see the results of our witness on the college campus.

In one sense, it is not up to us to bring men to Christ but to bring Christ to men. It is up to us to be faithful stewards. Man can resist God's call to salvation, but when he does come to faith in Christ, it is God who has converted him.

Let us be faithful in our task as witnesses. God's Word will do its own work.

Patience

READ ROMANS 8

"Let us run with patience the race that is set before us," the campus pastor intoned from the pulpit. "We glory in tribulations also, knowing that tribulation worketh patience; and patience, experience . . . ."

The student squirmed in his pew. "That may be O. K. for you," he thought to himself, "but not for me. Patience! Endurance! I've *had* it this semester!"

But the campus pastor was right — rather, the Scripture was right — in saying that the testing of our faith, hard and difficult as it may be to bear, is God's way of perfecting us and equipping us for better service to Him.

A woman, a former surgeon on the staff of the hospital where she now lay as a patient, told me, "This may sound strange to you, Pastor, but I thank God for giving me tuberculosis these last thirty months. In the last ten years, although I was brought up in the church, I had totally forgotten about God in my daily life. Lying on my back these many months has given me plenty of opportunity to re-examine my faith and to get my feet planted again, with God's help, on the road back to God."

Thank God for tuberculosis? It sounds strange, but perhaps the secret is locked up in the rest of the passage to which the student was reacting so negatively: "We glory in tribulations also, knowing that tribulation worketh patience; and patience, experience; and experience, hope; and hope maketh not ashamed *because the love of God is shed abroad in our hearts by the Holy Ghost, which is given unto us.*" (Romans 5:3-5 KJV)

Ah, there is the key! The love of God will give us the gift of patience. God knows what He is doing, even though we cannot understand it now.

A Wealthy Father

READ EPHESIANS 1

A young Japanese exchange student, who had been a Christian for only a few years, once told me something I have never forgotten. He stayed in International House, near the campus. In the elevator one day another foreign student, a chance acquaintance of his but not a Christian, remarked to him: "You must have a very wealthy father back home. You are always smiling and seem so very happy."

"He did not know," said the young Christian quietly, "that when I became a Christian I lost my family and my friends; my father cut me off from our family because I had left the religion of my ancestors." He mused a minute, then went on: "I could have told him that the only wealthy father I had was my Father who is in heaven, and the riches of His grace alone have made it possible for me to be a Christian in spite of all the loneliness I have suffered since being cut off from my relatives."

Here indeed was living proof of God's promise that He will be with all those in loneliness and despair, even in heartache such as this, when one has been cut off from his own parents. And this young Japanese Christian lived out God's promise and truth in his life. He was an avid witness for his faith on the campus, a living testimony that God's promises work.

In him the promise of the apostle Paul to the

Philippian Christians came true: "My God will supply every need of yours according to His riches in glory in Christ Jesus."

The glorious truth is that these riches can be the prize and treasure of every one of us. "In Him we have redemption through His blood, the forgiveness of our trespasses, according to the riches of His grace which He lavished upon us." (Ephesians 1:7)

READ LUKE 17

One of the oldest criticisms raised against the church is expressed in the comment: "I don't want to have anything to do with the church; I know too many hypocrites who are in it."

The response of a Christian to this comment is the frank admission that there are hypocrites in the church. But beyond the quip, "Come on in, there is always room for one more," it should also be pointed out that there is hardly an organization, a profession, an occupation of any kind which does not have its share of hypocrites.

Two thousand years ago the Bible itself made it clear that "church walls don't make a Christian." Our blessed Lord told the Pharisees in Luke 17:20: "The kingdom of God is not coming with signs to be observed; nor will they say, 'Lo here it is!' or, 'There!' For behold, the kingdom of God is in the midst of you."

The appeal that we must make to the critic of the church, the one hesitant to enter its portals for systematic examination of the Christian religion, is to look not just at the often bad carbon copies of Christ but at Christ Himself. It must be our challenge to them that they look not just at the organization but at the organism; not just at the denomination but at that living dynamic which is the kingdom of God.

A businessman once spoke to a group of his colleagues and asked them to list their criticisms of Christianity. He listened for an hour as they spelled out their complaints. At the end of that time he said, "You know, all of your criticisms have been against the church and the human beings which make it up. None of you had any complaint to make about Christ. Now let me tell you about Him."

"Why Is God Doing This to Me?"

READ JAMES 1

The Christian schoolteacher felt he had done a fine job with the seventh and eighth grades as they discussed the topic of temptation. He had made a careful distinction between the words "test" and "tempt," pointing out that often when the Bibles uses the word "tempt" the real meaning behind the Greek word is a testing of one's faith. And the class, he felt, understood that God always gives an individual the strength he needs to bear the burden placed on his shoulders, and the grace to overcome all evil with God's help.

"Are there any questions?" said the teacher as he wrapped up the lesson. A hand slowly rose in the back row, and an eighth-grade boy said, "Well, teacher, I know that God doesn't make us do evil. And I know that He only tests our faith to give us a chance to grow stronger as His children. But, you know, I still think that sometimes He overdoes it."

Some of the greatest minds in history have in effect said the same thing, like the philosopher who said, "If there is a God, He is to be blamed for giving me my reason with which I now reject Him."

But whatever the objection to God or His plan for our lives or the tests and tribulations of faith which He permits to enter the daily run of our affairs, the problem is not that God does not make Himself discoverable or make His help available to us. Rather it is that we do not really believe the mighty promises of God. We don't really make use of the tools of Word and Sacrament by which He would apply His power, His strength, and His peace to our lives.

No, we have "a God who is faithful." And He has promised us that if we will but "seek the Lord while He may be found" (Isaiah 55:6), we will find the way of escape that we may be "able to endure it." (1 Corinthians 10:13)

Big Deal!

READ PSALM 31

The co-ed was so sincere as she explained her intentions to the campus pastor. "I love that fellow so much, I'd just give anything if he'd ask me to marry him. I have prayed to God every night for weeks now that He would move that man in my life to ask me to marry him. If God could let that happen, I would be the best Christian you've ever seen. I would be in the front row of church every Sunday for the rest of my life— my family and my children. This is so right for me! If God will help me out on this thing, I promise God I'll be faithful to Him all the rest of my life."

Does one make "deals" with God? Is the Christian faith a matter of doing nice things for God because He has given us what we want? Even the word "gratitude," which we often use, may well leave some people with the impression that we in effect say to God, "Thank You, God, for all the nice things You've done for me; now look at the nice things I'm going to do for You." One wonders what this young woman would have done if God did not answer her prayers. Would she then be justified in feeling that God didn't really love her? Was she then somehow absolved from a faithful life of service to Christ? And if the handsome man in her life had married her, just what kind of worship of God would it have been as she sat in that front pew every Sunday morning?

114

Our prayer should not be: "Lord, give me this, and then I'll do that for You." Rather: "Thank You, God, for my salvation and all the other wonderful things You have given me without measure. I want to learn cheerfully to accept what You give. Give me that grace."

My Needs?—
Or What I *Need* to Hear?

READ PSALM 12

In *The Churchman and the Social Sciences* Warren H. Schmidt makes the point that man is a need-meeting being and that the church should take this into account as it brings its message to modern man.

One can immediately see the dangers that are implicit in the church simply seeking to adjust its message and its program to the *needs* of men and women. The extreme of this approach in present-day churches has led to a loss of sound theology, to a "psychologizing" of the Gospel, and to turning the church into an agency that simply tells man what he wants to hear or helps him get ahead in business or solve his marital problems.

But Schmidt carefully avoids these traps and still makes helpful use of the insights of the social sciences in telling us about man psychologically and in relationship to other men sociologically.

He points out that God has placed the need for security within us, and to this the Christian Gospel has said, "You are safe. This is God's world, and He loves you."

Man's need for self-respect is demonstrated in the individual being told of his importance to God, how God "spared not His own Son but delivered Him up for us all." Here indeed is reason for self-respect, when one knows that he is loved as God's own child.

And the need or drive for self-development and achievement is fulfilled in the Great Commission, which directs and empowers a man to live a creative, service-centered life.

No, the church of God does not simply feed the self-centered needs of pagan man; but it is aware of the nature of man, and the all-encompassing Gospel speaks to man in his every need and condition.

Our Guilt or My Guilt?

READ ROMANS 2

The contemporary novel written by a perceptive literary artist has many values for the Christian. It gives him a better picture of the world he lives in, the world to which he is to communicate the Gospel; it gives him a deeper insight into the nature of other people; and it may even help him better understand himself as he identifies with a central character or a central thesis of the writer.

One Achilles' heel, however, which afflicts many a modern writer's work is that sin, evil, guilt, wrong are often viewed as a corporate condition, and therefore the individual is often not seen as wholly culpable as he should be. By clever dialog and developed polemic, whatever guilt an individual has is seen as "the state of us all." And in such a case one's radical personal sin (and any admission of rebellion against God) is minimized or glossed over.

Joel H. Nederhood has pointed out the result of this treatment in noting that the doctrine of original sin has actually become the great equalizer: "It provides all men with a perfect excuse for their sinfulness." And Edmund Fuller has further described the philosophy in the words: "Neither do I condemn you; go and sin some more."

But Scripture is penetratingly and incisively clear that sin is a personal offense against a just and holy God. And although each individual, like a shoot in a strawberry patch, is connected with other runners and the parent stock, beyond original sin and corruption there is personal, individual culpability for one's transgressions against the holy Law of God.

Thus David said: "Against Thee, Thee only have I sinned and done that which is evil in Thy sight" (Psalm 51:4). And the apostle Paul told the Romans: "So each of us shall give account of himself to God." (Romans 14:12)

Indeed, although we are saved solely by the grace of God, the Scripture abounds with references which demonstrate that man is personally "accountable" before God for his own life.

J. B. Phillips put it aptly in his paraphrase of Romans 6:23: "Sin *pays* its servants: the wage is death. But God *gives* to those who serve Him: His free gift is eternal life through Jesus Christ, our Lord."

The Ethical or the Ontological?

It has been said that there was no "new" false doctrine to come into the church after the end of the 4th century. By that time just about every heresy that was possible, in one variety or another, had cropped up in the young church.

No doubt the questions that man has asked about the meaning of existence and his own nature down through history have already been asked years before by philosophers and all those in quest of man's destiny. Indeed, as Ecclesiastes says: "Is there a thing of which it is said, 'See, this is new'? It has been already, in the ages before us." (Ecclesiastes 1:10)

Nevertheless, at this point in history perhaps a certain type of question is being asked by the man of this world with an intensity not typical of earlier times. A century ago a man may have asked, "Why doesn't God *show* His love to me more?" Later the question came: "Is God a *loving* God?" Then came the question: "*Is* there a God?"

But today many people are asking: "Is the question: 'Is there a God?' a relevant question?"

The Christian must deal with the questions which the man of this day is asking. He must "start where he is" and take seriously the concerns and queries which come from the people of our age.

But at the same time the man in search of himself is often asking the wrong questions.

120

Ultimately the Scriptural dictum must be voiced firm and clear: "The fool says in his heart, 'There is no God'" (Psalm 53:1). "Be still, and know that I am God," says the Creator of man. When Job in his suffering cries out to God, "Show me my guilt, O God," God in effect implies that Job is asking the wrong question. For the Almighty Creator of all the universes asks the question: "Where were you when . . . ?" Then follows the whole catalog of creation in the stirring chapters, Job 38—42.

Indeed, "it is He that hath made us, and not we ourselves" (Psalm 100:3 KJV). Even as the clay does not point out to the potter the shape it will take, so the Scripture reminds us, "Ye are not your own." "For ye are bought with a price; therefore glorify God in your body and in your spirit, which are God's." (1 Corinthians 6:20 KJV)

Man the creature has often made himself into the creator and therefore is asking the wrong questions. When we in Scripture find the answer as to who we are and where we are going, then we can ask the right questions—and find their answers in the life and person and work of the great God-man, Jesus Christ, for it is in Him that we are to live and move and have our being.

"Try It! — You'll Like It!"

READ JOHN 7

Coleridge was once asked, "Is Christianity true?" His terse reply was, "Try it!" The Christian faith can stand the test. John 7:17 (KJV) says: "If any man will do His will, he shall know of the doctrine, whether it be of God."

The Christian religion gives its own unique "evidence" and "proof." It is true not because it is something that a person has been brought up in, but because *God is true* — for all of us!

Because God the Father is true (and not just because people have wanted and desired the idea of a god), His mighty acts are visible in the affairs of men all down through history.

Because Jesus Christ is true, He demonstrated the truth and the power of His love by His sacrificial death for us and His miraculous resurrection from the dead, being God Himself.

Because the Holy Spirit of God is true, He has come and continues to come into our hearts, showing over and over again that the God who created us and continues to support our life, forgives our sins and gives us the power to remain His sons and as remade people lets us start life each day anew.

So to those who question the integrity and authenticity of the Christian religion we say, "Try it! It works." Use the tools by which God reveals Himself to man, and you will have all the "evidence" and all the "proof" that you need.

"But I'm Not Hurting Anyone Else!"

READ 1 CORINTHIANS 6

In a stage play which depicts the story of the life of Joseph in the Old Testament, the temptress at one point tears off her skirt and throws it over the bust of a pagan god in the corner. At this point she calls to Joseph and bewitchingly says, "Now God will not see."

But to this Joseph firmly replies, "But my God sees!"

How does one conduct his sexuality wisely? Is it a matter of knowing that God "sees" all the time, and therefore in fear of a just and wrathful God we go only as far as God's Ten Commandments permit us to go in our relationship with a person of the opposite sex?

God's judgment certainly does come upon those who break His law. Scripture says: "Avoid immorality. Any other sin a man commits does not affect his body; but the man who commits immorality sins against his own body. Don't you know that your body is the temple of the Holy Spirit, who lives in you, the Spirit given you by God? You do not belong to yourselves but to God; He bought you for a price. So use your bodies for God's glory." (1 Corinthians 6:18-20 TEV)

There is also a positive note in this passage of Scripture. The approach to the problem of conduct of one's sexuality is not only a matter of "Don't do this! Don't do that!" Rather it is a blessed realization that one's body is a gift from

God and that the Holy Spirit of God Himself reigns within. It involves the holy awareness of the fact that this body was bought with a price, the price of Christ's own death on the cross. Therefore the Christian, knowing of the great love of Christ for him, doesn't just avoid certain things but rather positively does that in his life which is pleasing to God.

You Are Four People

READ PSALM 116

It has been said that each of us really has four selves. First of all there is your inner self, that self which is known only to you and to God. This is the self which is deep down in your heart; it is your "true" self.

Then there is your self which is your mask to the world: what you see on the faces of other people every day, the way they look to you—and the way you look to them.

Then, third, there is the self that you "ought" to be. And finally, there is the self that you'd like to be.

From the Christian perspective, of course, there may be a big difference between the self that one would like to be and the self that one ought to be. Christ may have very different plans for our personality, and what He would do with our life, than what we would like to do. We may often misunderstand the words of the psalmist: "Take delight in the Lord, and He will give you the desires of your heart" (Psalm 37:4). This doesn't mean that God will give us what we want—or the "self" that we would like—but that rather He will put the right desires into our hearts.

Yes, there's a big gap, a big difference, between the first self of the true nature of our heart and the self that we ought to be under God. Christ is the One who "makes" the difference. He takes

125

over our whole being, and it becomes His temple. Indeed, He has already begun His great work through the Sacrament of Holy Baptism and through the life-giving forgiveness of sins which is ours through faith in Christ.

This is our prayer:

> Finish, then Thy new creation;
> Pure and spotless let us be.
> Let us see Thy great salvation
> Perfectly restored in Thee . . .

Isolation — Acceptance — Relationship

The words of the psych lab can be very helpful to Christian students in communicating the meaning and relevance of Christian faith for contemporary man.

"Isolation" is certainly a word that modern man understands. Loneliness is still the biggest problem that plagues all of us, and even in the teeming masses of society we are "lost in the lonely crowd." The root problem, of course, is our isolation from God until we come to know Jesus Christ and fall in love with Him.

"Acceptance." Think of this word not just as the acceptance of a body of dogma as being true but as the realization that we have been declared "accepted" by God the Father, even though we are "unacceptable." Through the work of Christ we can really learn to "accept" other people, no matter how unlovely they may be. For because of Christ's work we ourselves have been made "acceptable" before God.

"Relationship." The Christian faith is not a matter of intellectually assenting to certain truths about God; it is not just a matter of keeping a certain set of Biblical rules. It is a living, breathing, growing, dynamic relationship with God through our Lord and Savior Jesus Christ.

So there we have it. Man without Christ is in isolation from God; His original sin and his

127

actual sin have separated him from his God. He is a person "having no hope and without God in the world." (Ephesians 2:12)

The doctrines of justification by faith in Christ and conversion by the work of the Holy Spirit are implicit in "acceptance." As Paul told the Roman Christians: "The kingdom of God [means] righteousness and peace and joy in the Holy Spirit; he who thus serves Christ is acceptable to God and approved by men" (Romans 14:17-18). We are "accepted in the Beloved." (Ephesians 1:6 KJV)

In the life of sanctification — that blessed work of the Holy Spirit, of our growing in grace steadily through the use of God's holy Word and His blessed sacraments — is found our "relationship" with God in His own family. Indeed, He is our closest "relative" — He is our heavenly Father. (Romans 8:15-16)

Out of darkness into light into daily growth in the fellowship with all the saints in God's family — thanks be to God for our salvation!

"I Am Free!"

READ GALATIANS 5

Several co-eds from different schools were chattering away as they traveled home for a Christmas vacation. They were comparing the various rules that their schools had set up in their dormitories, rules that had to be observed or severe penalties would be imposed. The girls compared the schools' differing regulations on how many rules could be broken before a person was "campused" for some time. They all agreed, of course, that there were entirely too many rules, and in general rebelled against what they thought gave them a "hemmed-in feeling."

The Christian religion may be viewed as a very narrow-minded religion, with all kinds of rules which tie down the individual and inhibit the development of one's own personality. God does have His "rules," His commandments and His whole Law for man's life. He has made us, and it is only right that He should expect us to live according to His way.

But Christianity is more than "living by the rules." To be a Christian is not just "to keep the Ten Commandments." Rather it is a matter of walking "by the Spirit" (Galatians 5:16). We who are "in Christ" are no longer "under the Law" but are now abounding in the good works which Christ produces in and through us.

Paul described it this way in speaking to the

Galatian Christians as he spoke of the liberty of the Gospel:

"But the Spirit produces love, joy, peace, patience, kindness, goodness, faithfulness, humility, and self-control. There is no law against such things as these. And those who belong to Christ Jesus have put to death their human nature, with all its passions and desires. The Spirit has given us life; He must also control our lives." (Galatians 5:22-25 TEV)

Think about it. Is your concept of the Christian faith a matter of "do this" and "don't do that"? Or, positively speaking, is it a matter of being a "little Christ" in all that you do, and being a channel of God's Holy Spirit at work in you producing this great list of "fruits of the Spirit"?

"Here Lies—"

READ MATTHEW 6

Christmas vacation was over, and the sophomore walked into her bedroom to start the job of packing to go back to school. She opened her suitcase on the bed, and there they were—the heavy stack of books she had lugged all the way home but hadn't "cracked" once. "Here lies good intention No. 8,563," she mused wistfully to herself.

"Don't do today what you can put off until tomorrow." There are just so many things to occupy one's time during the fast-moving collegiate days that often the greatest, most vital tasks remain undone. But all the promises in the world are going to mean nothing unless results come from them.

All promises to God—improving our spiritual life with more regular and meaningful Bible study, prayerfully preparing for and making use of Holy Communion whenever it is offered, really making use of the witness opportunities which God has placed all around us on campus—are but hollow phrases if we don't follow through on them. Indeed, Scripture includes a note of warning and serious judgment on those who say one thing to God and do another. "This people honors Me with their lips, but their heart is far from Me." (Matthew 15:8)

How can one change? Try this, and pray over it. As each morning begins, meditate on the

Christ who gave His love and life for the student caught in unfulfilled good intentions. Say to yourself, "This day will be spent for Jesus Christ." Check your progress at noon, later in the day, and then before going to sleep say one of two things — really being honest with yourself: "This day was spent for Jesus Christ," or: "Little was done for Jesus Christ."

"God-Shelf"?

READ 1 TIMOTHY 2

A foreign student had been in the home of a Christian girl friend over the Christmas vacation. Before leaving for school, the girl's mother asked the international student if she had enjoyed her stay with them. To this the young girl, not a Christian, replied: "Yes, I enjoy my stay very much. But one thing puzzles me. You not have God-shelf in your home? In my country everybody have God-shelf in their house. You worship your God only in church?"

It is an incisive question. Many pagan religions make quite a bit of having a small shrine in the home around which the family gathers for prayers to their pagan gods. So many Christians still have very few things in their homes which are symbolic of the Christian life and of the center of the Christian faith, our Lord and Savior and His cross.

What is there in your study room to let others know that you are a Christian? How might you make use of works of art which would not only declare to others the Christ whom you love and serve but also be rich stimulation for your meditation and a reminder of Him whose you are and whom you serve?

We need to say with the disciples, "Lord, teach us to pray" (Luke 11:1). For we "ought always to pray" (Luke 18:1). We should be "praying always with all prayer and supplication in

the Spirit and watching thereunto with all per-
severance and supplication for all saints."
(Ephesians 6:18 KJV)

We are to "pray without ceasing" (1 Thessalonians 5:17 KJV) and "pray everywhere, lifting
up holy hands without wrath and doubting."
(1 Timothy 2:8 KJV)

Is there a "God-shelf" where you live? How
might you better enhance the "room of your
mind"?

"I Vant To Be Alone"

READ PSALM 130

Greta Garbo said it: "I vant to be alone." Many a college student has responded in the same tone to the well-intentioned invitation of Christian students to visit their campus church. Those invited often make it clear they want to have nothing to do with religion, in some cases will even write bitter letters of protest to campus churches that put them on their mailing list. And on the registration card at the beginning of the school year such a student may make the entries: "Race—human; Church preference—Gothic."

Man by nature wants to be left alone by God and by His representatives. This is the nature of sin—"wanting to be independent from God." And we can see how utterly "logical" it is from God's point of view: "My child, if you insist on living independent of Me and My will for your life here on the earth, then I must make it an eternal separation from Me in the life that is to come."

A Christian psychiatrist once put it this way: "Man's basic problem is still loneliness. This stems from man's 'original sin' of self-imposed loneliness and isolation from God back in the Garden of Eden."

We can leave the loving care of our heavenly Father—fall away from faith. But no one can snatch us out of God's protecting hand—"Who, then, can separate us from the love of Christ? Can trouble do it, or hardship, or persecution, or hunger, or poverty, or danger, or death? No, in all these things we have complete victory through Him who loved us! For I am certain that nothing can separate us from His love: neither death nor life; neither angels nor other heavenly rulers or powers; neither the present nor the future; neither the world above nor the world below—there is nothing in all creation that will ever be able to separate us from the love of God which is ours through Christ Jesus our Lord." (Romans 8:35, 37-39)

"Nod-to-God Week"

READ ACTS 22

Religious Emphasis or Religion in Life Weeks have often been disparagingly called "Nod-to-God Weeks." Some have suggested that to give a halfhearted nod to religion during only one such week is about as innocuous and idiotic as having a Chemistry Emphasis Week or Physics Emphasis Week only once during the year.

But such weeks can still present good opportunities at times for a witness to Christ's Gospel. Take for example the Christian professor at Iowa State who introduced me to a hundred freshman girls in his economics class, saying, "I want you to know that I am very happy to introduce this man to you. Many of my colleagues, together with me, feel that the spiritual values of life are very important in the student's academic life. In fact, I spend every Saturday evening preparing for the Bible class which I teach in my local church on Sunday morning. And so I am happy to welcome this guest speaker to our class during this week, to heighten the need for one's spiritual orientation through all of the courses which one takes on campus."

Some professors would violently criticize a statement like this, indeed would question the man's "right" to say it. As Joel H. Nederhood comments in his *The Church's Mission to the Educated American:* "Apparently, the neutrality and the objectivity which governs so much of

137

academic life becomes operative whenever one is biased in favor of Christianity; it does not seem to operate when one is biased against it." (Page 74)

Christian students and Christian professors need to encourage one another to be bold like the apostles in making clear their Christian convictions, just as the naturalist and the secularist are bold in their so-called "objectivity." This is not to call for illegal indoctrination of Christian truths in college courses but rather to note the legitimacy of stating one's own view when the proper time presents itself. For God's call is a strong one: "You will be a witness for Him to all men of what you have seen and heard" (Acts 22:15). "We are witnesses to these things, and so is the Holy Spirit, whom God has given to those who obey Him." (Acts 5:32)

The "things" of which we are not afraid to speak? "You denied the Holy and Righteous One . . . and killed the Author of life, whom God raised from the dead. To this we are witnesses." (Acts 3:14-15)

READ PSALM 86

He was a good-looking physics student, and two co-eds, good dormitory pals, thought he was just about the "most." He had been dating both of them off and on; indeed, the dating process had almost moved into the courtship stage.

That night one of the girls prayed to God, "Dear God, I love him so much! Please move him in his heart to see me as his life's partner, so that he will ask me to marry him before I go crazy with all this waiting. I love You, God, and I love him too. Please help me." And the other girl—well, she prayed exactly the same prayer!

Now what in the world was God supposed to do? Here the two of His children, both faithful Christians, and they prayed the same prayer to God over the same young man. God is "on the fence"—how does He decide this one?

Well, of course, the big thing that is missing in the prayer is the phrase without which you don't have a Christian prayer at all: "O, Lord, not my will but Thine be done."

We need to learn the blessing—yes, the blessing—of *un*answered prayer. God knows far better than we do what is best for us. For our prayers can often be wrong prayers and actually should not be answered by our loving God. Our prayers can be wrong when we try to get God on our side in a quarrel or disagreement and try to justify something which is not defensible. Or our prayers can be wrong when we try to get God's support for our own carefully laid plans rather than His guidance for what He knows would be best.

God loves us. He knows what He is doing in our lives. How can He "go wrong"? Your heavenly Father knows what you need. Trust Him!

The Poli-Sci Prof Eye-Batter

READ PSALM 42

A student once noted that his political science professor had batted his eyes 70 times in 60 seconds. No doubt this was distracting; we also wonder how much the student got out of what the professor was saying.

Distractions of one kind or another can be a real impediment to a Christian student's prayer and worship life. We remember the story of the Polish juggler who after an airplane crash wanted to make sure he had full coordination. He was relieved when he could read Psalm 23 aloud without a hitch while juggling six oranges at the same time.

Many of us read the Bible that way, or sit in the pew in church, look at the altar or at the pastor in the pulpit while we are mentally busy with the term paper for Monday morning, the ironing which is still to be done for the big date, or the processing of any other baggage in our mind which may pop up into our consciousness.

Scripture urges: "Therefore we must pay the closer attention to what we have heard lest we drift away from it" (Hebrews 2:1). Scripture urges us to "attend to the voice" of God, to "attend to His words," to "give attendance to reading," and to give attendance at God's altar.

Then when we pray: "O Lord, let Thy ear be attentive to the prayer of Thy servant and to the prayer of Thy servants who delight to fear Thy name; and give success to Thy servant today, and grant him mercy in the sight of this man" (Nehemiah 1:11) — when we ask for God's attention to our prayers, the joyous fact is that He has promised to hear us. "If My people who are called by My name humble themselves and pray and seek My face and turn from their wicked ways, then I will hear from heaven and will forgive their sin and heal their land." (2 Chronicles 7:14)

The Laws of Learning

READ PSALM 33

Students in the school of education become quite familiar with the "laws of learning."

One way of stating them is:

The law of readiness—the learner must be motivated to learn by taking into account physical considerations, the interests of the individual, his emotional needs, and using the principle of "proceeding from the known to the unknown."

The law of satisfaction or effect—the pupil must see a satisfying purpose for the material in his own life.

The law of exercise—hardly a spectator, the pupil must put into practice what has been learned.

The law of belonging or association—the material must be seen in relationship to the total body of subject matter.

One can quickly see the relevance of these "laws of learning" to one's practicing of the Christian faith. Man certainly is "ready" for the message of God's law and then that of the forgiveness of sins in the Gospel; if a man is not deceiving himself, he is aware of his sin and his radical dislocation from God, and his need for "being made right with God" (justification by faith).

The law of satisfaction or effect is applicable in the joy that the Christian has in his new relationship in Christ. He sees God at work in his own life and, together with the many expressions of confidence and exhilaration found throughout the psalms, says with the psalmist: "Our heart is glad in Him because we trust in His holy name." (Psalm 33:21)

The law of exercise immediately calls to mind the words of the apostle Paul: "And so I do my best always to have a clear conscience before God and men" (Acts 24:16 TEV). The Christian puts into practice what he has learned; it's not only "head knowledge" but the service of our whole being lived out in daily life.

The law of belonging or association? Whatever aspect of our blessed Lord's life and work we might consider, we see it all culminating in His greatest miracle of all, His resurrection from the grave. Every aspect of Christian doctrine focuses in the death and resurrection of Jesus Christ — the central doctrine of being justified — "being made right in God's eyes" — solely through faith in the meritorious work of our Savior. So the Christian rejoices in the promise: "If you confess with your lips that Jesus is Lord and believe in your heart that God raised Him from the dead, you will be saved." (Romans 10:9)

Spaghetti Suppers

READ PHILIPPIANS 3

The president of the Sunday evening student fellowship was thanking the local ladies' aid for the fine meal they had prepared for the students. "It was really wonderful to get a good home-cooked meal for a change," he said, "not like the spaghetti we usually get here every Sunday night." And then a look of dismay came over his face as he remembered that the ladies' aid also had fixed spaghetti for the students.

For some strange reason the word "fellowship" has come to be associated with the eating of a lot of food. Read the word "fellowship" in a church bulletin, and a vision of an endlessly long table laden with hot dishes, salads, and desserts comes to mind. Further, the comment might be made in a church, "We've got to have more fellowship around here!" And somebody starts planning dinners, or at least gatherings at which people are supposed to get acquainted and feel "real good" together.

The New Testament concept of fellowship is radically, totally different. Far from being a stomach-serving operation, fellowship is not even a "good spirit" that you "work for." Rather, in the Scriptural sense of the term, fellowship is something Christians already have. It is that deep spiritual kinship which all Christians have together in Christ, based on that once-for-all act which He accomplished for all men by His death on the cross.

Every person who is a baptized Christian is in this state already. Indeed, he has been in it for many, many years, even as the redemption of the whole world has been an accomplished fact for many years. "To me," said the apostle Paul to the Ephesians, "though I am the very least of all the saints, this grace was given, to preach to the Gentiles the unsearchable riches of Christ and to make all men see what is the plan of the mystery hidden for ages in God, who created all things." (Ephesians 3:8-9)

This is a "fellowship in the Gospel from the first day until now" (Philippians 1:5 KJV). This is a "fellowship of the Spirit" of God (Philippians 2:1 KJV). Indeed, this is a fellowship of the sons of God who already live as redeemed beings in God's kingdom and don't have to "work for more fellowship around here." For we say with the apostle Paul that our desire is that "I may know Him and the power of His resurrection and the fellowship of His sufferings, being made conformable unto His death, if by any means I might attain unto the resurrection of the dead." (Philippians 3:10-11 KJV)

And so when we invite someone to the student chapel for "fellowship," it's not just because the dormitory doesn't have a Sunday evening dinner but because we are inviting these people to the eternal fellowship of God in Christ Jesus. "That which we have seen and heard declare we unto you, that ye also may have fellowship with us;

and truly our fellowship is with the Father and with His Son Jesus Christ." (1 John 1:3 KJV)

This is the whole purpose of any gathering in the student chapel or student center: "If we walk in the light, as He is in the light, we have fellowship one with another, and the blood of Jesus Christ, His Son, cleanseth us from all sin." (1 John 1:7 KJV)

Philosophy, Not Science

READ PSALM 100

A pastor was inviting a lady to bring her spouse to the services at the campus chapel. To this the young woman replied, "Oh, my husband is a scientist. And of course he doesn't believe in God."

To this the pastor quietly replied, "That's not science; that's philosophy."

Science per se has nothing to do with the question of whether there is or is not a God. A scientist himself may not believe that there is a God, but that is his own subjective view. The task of science is not to deal with the moral or ethical values of life; that is the task and role of philosophy.

So it does not follow that if one is scientific, he therefore would reject the idea of God. Indeed, it would be much closer to the task of science in one sense to grant the limitations of scientific method and to be constantly open to the discovery of new truths – truths far above and beyond that which we now know with our limited discoveries.

To the one who rejects the idea of God the Christian student says, "Come now, let us be scientific about it. Let us make a thorough and systematic examination of the claims of the Christian religion."

So spoke the Old Testament prophet Isaiah: "Come now, let us reason together, says the Lord: though your sins are like scarlet, they shall be as white as snow; though they are red like crimson, they shall become like wool" (Isaiah 1:18). And the daring promise of Scripture is always fulfilled to those who would truly be open-minded in their investigation of Christ and His doctrine: "If any man will do His will, he shall know of the doctrine, whether it be of God." (John 7:17 KJV)

"Come now, let's be scientific about it!"

Are You Bold?

READ 1 JOHN 5

The one agnostic was puzzled as he said to his fellow doubter, "Why do you go to hear that fellow preach all the time? You don't believe the stuff that he says, do you?"

"No," said his friend in reply, "but he does."

The preacher they were referring to was unashamed of preaching the Gospel of Jesus Christ. Yet it was not a Gospel of his own making, nor did he have a power from within himself that caused the one doubter to come back again and again to hear what he had to say. We recall the example in the Book of Acts when two of our Lord's disciples were fulfilling the missionary calling with which the Lord had entrusted them, and the Scripture says: "Now when they saw the boldness of Peter and John and perceived that they were uneducated, common men, they wondered; and they recognized that they had been with Jesus" (Acts 4:13). Like worshipers in one ancient Eastern city who had been to a temple the interior of which was filled with burning incense, and who leaving the temple carried the sweet odor with them wherever they went (so that people could tell that they had been to the temple) — so the disciples of Christ bore on them the mark of the great God-man Jesus Christ. It was His powerful message that they declared, and it was from Him that they received the strength for their boldness.

Knowing that God was with them, these men could say, as we can today: "Be content with what you have; for He has said, 'I will never fail you nor forsake you.' So we can confidently say, 'The Lord is my Helper, I will not be afraid; what can man do to me?'" (Hebrews 13:5-6)

Because Christ was God in the flesh, with our heavenly Father's own Word of truth for man, they said of Him, "No man ever spoke like this man!" (John 7:46). And so the world says of us as we speak Christ's Gospel with all boldness, "He really believes that, you know?" And this is true, for the Scripture promises: "He who believes in the Son of God has the testimony in himself. He who does not believe God has made Him a liar because he has not believed in the testimony that God has borne to His Son. And this is the testimony, that God gave us eternal life, and this life is in His Son." (1 John 5:10-11)

As Christ, therefore, is seen alive and at work in His children, His promise comes true: "And I, when I am lifted up from the earth, will draw all men to Myself." (John 12:32)

Thank You!

READ PSALM 136

Thank You, God, for searching me out when I was running the opposite direction away from You and calling me back into the circle of Your family even though I didn't deserve Your forgiveness. Thank You, God, for directing my attention away from myself and to my Savior, my Lord Jesus Christ, who has loved me and given me His own life's blood that I might be His own and live under Him in His kingdom.

Thank You, God, for my parents. I may not know all that they have done to make my education possible or, even beyond the material help they have given me, the concern and the prayers which they constantly have for me even though they may be many miles away.

Thank You, God, for my fellow students. Thank You for those who have been of special help to me in so many little ways during these rigorous days of campus life. Yes, thank You, God, also for those whose personality has been in such contrast to mine; I have learned from them the need to be loving, and I have seen the opportunity to be serving — to those so very different from me that whenever I serve someone else I am really serving You.

Thank You, God, for all of my teachers. I haven't always appreciated everything they have done either, but they are really Your gift to me, I know, and I want to thank You now for all the inspiration and instruction and insights which they have transmitted to me from the great lore of history and current thought.

Thank You, God, for all the other people on campus who make my life here possible—those who serve the meals, those who keep the buildings clean, all the secretaries and other non-academic personnel without whom this school would not be able to run.

Thank You, God, for the fellowship of other Christians on this campus. I really need my fellow saints, indeed must confess that I have not sought the fellowship of my brothers and sisters in Christ as often as I ought. Thank You, God, for Your church, for all its sources of power and comfort which are found in Christ, its Head. Thank You, God, for the gift of mind and body such as I have. Please, help me to use the talents that You have given me to the best of my ability and not to be discontent because I have not the talents that some of Your other children have.

Thank You, God, for all the many gifts which You have poured into my life without number, the likes of which I cannot begin to name right now. Truly, You are a great and living God, and I owe You all that I am and have.

Thank You, God!

Catching the Vision

READ EPHESIANS 5

Is there "love in your life"? Whether you are just dating someone, are deep in a rich and meaningful courtship, or are a married student, just how do you view your relationship with the other person?

Certainly all of us want to be loved, and we need the love and affection of another person. Yet this is only part, a small part of a romantic relationship.

Well, then, let's say that to love the other person must certainly be the highest goal and end of our relationship. To deny ourselves, to give ourselves to and for them, certainly this is the noble goal of two Christians in their courtship or dating relationship and then in that noble estate called holy matrimony.

But there is even more. Since there is always a third partner where a Christian man and woman are concerned, there is still another dimension involved where the two sexes meet. I am saying that the ultimate essence of your relationship with this other person is not only to be loved or to love but rather to catch God's vision of what the other person is to be, and to see your role in helping that other person achieve, in Christ, that high calling.

Did you ever think of the other person in that way? The dimension is not only horizontal, but it also involves the vertical, the other person's relationship with God. Everything that the two of you do together must be seen in this light: How can I help the other person achieve God's purpose in his or her life? How can I keep from forcing this other person into a mold, into a stereotype of someone I want to be a certain way and to treat me in a certain way and to love me in a certain way? And, beyond loving this person simply because I love her or him, how can I catch onto the vision of what God wants to achieve in that person's life?

This is the real purpose that God has in the relationship of a man and a woman together, both before marriage and in it. Everything is seen within the perspective of God's grace and His purpose, not just between the two people involved. This will also involve a total freeing of the other person — a freeing which is possible only if true love is there. Anne Morrow Lindbergh put it this way: "Him that I love I wish to be free — even from me."

Have you freed your partner — in love? Have you caught God's vision of what the other person can become?

"Publish or Perish!"

READ MARK 16

Two humanists were sitting in a Protestant church which had a large corpus of Christ above the altar.

The one mused to the other as he contemplated Christ on the cross. He said: "Ah, He was a great Teacher!"

"Yes," agreed the other, "too bad He never published!"

There is more behind the comments of these two men than the classic tension on a campus as to whether a prof is a good teacher or a good research man, one apt in the classroom or one who makes his primary contribution in laboratory discoveries or literary productions.

The blessed truth about our great Teacher is that He did "publish." He was not only Rabbi, Teacher, of His disciples and all who heard Him. He also published the Gospel, the Good News that He had come to seek and to save that which was lost. The news released at first went out to small groups of people in a small country. Then, after His resurrection and Pentecost, His reporters carried the message throughout the first-century world.

Later the finger of God wrote the New Testament through the apostles and evangelists. Centuries passed, and a Wittenberg professor published the news again in the language of his people. The news release spread again, throughout the 16-century world, "as if it had been borne on angels' wings," one historian wrote.

Today, through the mass media around the world, men in every clime, continent, and condition hear the headline story of Him who suffered and died and rose again that we might live with Him forever.

He was a great Teacher. And He also published.

Theocentric vs. Anthropocentric

READ DEUTERONOMY 6

In *The Church's Mission to the Educated American* Joel H. Nederhood makes three points in a section on "Preaching to the Educated": (1) It must be stressed that God is the Creator. (2) God is a God of judgment. (3) The Christian faith is relevant to the totality of one's life. These points are extremely significant and have one theme in common: theocentrism, that is, God-centeredness. This is in opposition to anthropocentrism, which points to man as the center of things.

Particularly in the field of higher education, where attention is focused on the world and the men in it, our concern must always be directed towards the Source, the Author and Finisher of all things—our majestic God.

Whatever job one has chosen in life, he should remember that God has made the world in which we live, and He alone gives the ability to work in it. This God will return to judge the world, indeed, has this world under judgment in a special sense right now. "He has showed you, O man, what is good; and what does the Lord require of you but to do justice and to love kindness and to walk humbly with your God?" (Micah 6:8)

Knowing this, there is not a corner of one's life in which God in Christ should not reign as Savior and King. For He is "Lord of all."

Do You Live in a Vacuum?

READ PSALM 150

In recent years the term "relationship" has come into vogue and has moved from the Psych classroom into common parlance in the mass media and daily conversation.

Christian educators have also coined a special usage of the term, speaking of a "theology of relationships." The point is made that the Christian faith has relevance and result only as it is worked out between people, that the faith is not an intangible thing but that it acts in the daily life situations — the relationships — of human beings. An extreme extension of this view has resulted in the "theology" of some groups which implies that religion emerges from people — from groups — and that where you have people who understand and love and accept one another, there you have religion, and "God" is at work.

The latter extreme view has been criticized by Christian theologians, however, who affirm that true religion does not ultimately come from men, no matter how loving they may be, but from God. Further, God's mediating grace is not dependent on people. People are rather a channel of His love and forgiveness and help to one another.

The faith of a Christian student on campus certainly expresses itself in relationship to other students. For one cannot be a Christian in a vacuum. Christianity is "social" in nature, and one needs other people to love, even as Christ loved us and gave Himself for us.

But the primary emphasis must never be shifted away from God—who He is and what He has done for our salvation. The thrust is on Him from whom all things come—the Creator, not the creatures; God, not groups.

The "Heresy of Paraphrase"

READ 2 JOHN

English Lit majors are familiar with the term "the heresy of paraphrase." In literary criticism, care is taken that concepts are not read into an author's work which are not really there. Nor should other value judgments inhibit considering a piece of work on its own grounds.

The Christian religion also should not be judged unfairly through the "heresy of paraphrase." An individual should not approach Scripture with his own preconceived opinions and prejudices. He should not make up his own self-satisfying religion and then look for a church or group which best fits it—and criticize all other forms of Christianity accordingly. In appraising the Christian faith, one should make sure it is Christianity one is evaluating, not a caricature of it.

In every instance one must be certain it is the true, genuine content of the Christian faith one is dealing with, not some substitute or counterfeit replica of it.

Even members of the Christian church themselves are not a completely adequate yardstick by which to assess the merits or demerits of Christianity as the true religion. For Christians, still being sinners, are only "carbon copies" of their Lord and Master Jesus Christ, and often poor "copies."

It is Christ to whom one must turn in examining the Christian faith if one is not to become guilty of the "heresy of paraphrase." It is in His nature, His person, and His work that one finds the answer as to what Christianity is and what it means to be a Christian. And, praise God, it is also in Him that one finds the power to be a "little Christ," one of the many "other Christs" living in the world before men.

"Objectives"

READ LUKE 10

An important task of the teacher-training student is to learn the art of formulating objectives. A precise statement of what is to be achieved in the learner is important before the selection of the method to be used in the learning process.

Many an education prof finds that his students state their goals only in terms of understandings, or attitudes, but not in terms of "patterns of action," that is, behavioral outcomes in the actual lives of the pupils. The former are important, but mental goals are limited in scope. More important is that an individual "learn by doing" and put theory into practice in the warp and woof of life.

Many a well-meaning young Christian has fallen into the trap of divorcing faith from life. When the fruits of Christian faith have been lacking, many a concerned parent or pastor has been told: "Oh, I still remember my catechism," or: "I still believe in the church's doctrines."

But there is a big difference between "head knowledge" and "heart knowledge." There is a world of difference between a mental assent to the truths of Scripture and a living out of the life of love and service and self-denial and witness to Christ among others.

As with the functional objectives of the educator, so the Christian faith must be lived out in one's life on campus.

Christ Himself set us the perfect example in

this respect. He was fully God, yet fully man. As a man He not only thought the right thing and prayed the right words but "did the will of His Father" in heaven.

"Never man spake like this man," said the Scripture. But words weren't enough for Christ. He did the Christian deed and actually lived each day in self-giving until the day He gave life itself on the cross.

"I just Couldn't Put It Down"

READ PSALM 19

The blond chemistry major left the sidewalk and approached the few students standing outside the campus chapel waiting for church services to begin. He wore large, dark glasses, which immediately caused sly comments from a number of his friends. "Ah, out on the town again late last night, eh, Paul?" said one of his buddies.

Paul smiled faintly, then commented: "No. You wouldn't believe this, but I was sitting in my room at International House last night preparing for Bible class this morning. If my eyes look tired, it's because I got to reading the Gospel of John in that new translation, and I just couldn't put it down!"

"He just couldn't put it down." How many of us have had the same experience? How many students give God much of a chance to speak to them through His Scriptures with an open mind and a ready heart?

This is not to imply that Bible reading in itself is a gimmick answer to one's problems, that some ecstatic experience can be expected, or even that Bible reading at first may not present more problems and questions than answers.

But God has promised that His Word doesn't return void, that those who seek Him will find Him, and that the earnest, penitent searching of this Scripture will equip a person to be "complete, equipped for every good work." (2 Timothy 3:16)

As one searches this Scripture, he will find "the Christ there cradled," as Luther put it, who will speak to him in his situation with His own love and mercy. No wonder that a person "just can't put it down." It affords the very lifestream of God Himself, where "men moved by the Holy Spirit spoke from God." (2 Peter 1:21)

A Faith to Live By

READ 1 TIMOTHY 1

The student sitting in the campus pastor's study was explaining the purpose for his visit. ". . . and I have no church background at all myself. So when I learned that my roommate is a member of your church, I wanted to find out more about it. Because, you see, that student really has a faith to live by. I want that faith!"

"A faith to live by." When one examines the phrase, it seems strange that "faith" could have any other meaning or use. But many students, when they are honest, must admit that their "faith" is not related to their life. It may be all "head knowledge" without "heart knowledge." "Faith" may have become a matter of believing the right doctrines or saying the proper prayers or "keeping the rules" of morality and ethics which one grew up with as a child.

But none of these are the Christian faith. For this faith is a living, dynamic life relationship with Christ. In the New Testament, faith involves not only knowledge but also assent and confidence, or trust. This faith pervades the totality of one's existence. It affects everything one does. It is at the root of all of life's relationships. For Christ, the Center of our faith, "is all and in all." (Colossians 3:11)

No wonder the student in the pastor's study was drawn to the life of his Christian roommate. For this one knew the Lord as his intimate

Friend and "lived Christ" in all that he did. This, in a nutshell, is what it means to "have" the Christian faith.

"And I, when I am lifted up from the earth," said our Lord, "will draw all men to Myself." (John 12:32)

"Why Is It?"

READ 1 THESSALONIANS 5

The guest chapel-speaker concluded his remarks. Then a student rose and spoke haltingly, almost painfully: "But if all that you say is true, sir, why is it that there are so few Christians around who really practice the Christian faith?"

It's quite a question, and a difficult one for any person to answer unless he gives a stock reply like: "Well, it's due to the perverse nature of man."

But look at the question again. Then look at what God has given to man.

Above all, He has given Himself into death for our sin. It is almost above human comprehension, such a gift of love. But God also grants the miraculous gift of faith, by which we can "understand" and practice His gracious presence in our lives.

But more! The charter of new life—my Holy Baptism, daily affirmed. The Scriptures—God's own message of life to me and in my language. The blessed Eucharist—His own body and blood, assuring me of the forgiveness of my sins. The church—fellow members of Christ's body to strengthen and sustain me and in whose fellowship I find joyous opportunity to serve Him and others. The life-giving channel of prayer and God's own tender admonition: "Ye have not because ye ask not." (Certainly our problem is not that God does not love us or help us but that we don't really believe the mighty promises of God.)

"Why is it that there are so few Christians who really practice the Christian faith?" It's quite a question. Is there an answer?

O Lord of my salvation, grant that I may use the precious gifts Thou hast given me to be a "little Christ" in all things.

"Biff—He Likes Me!"

READ PSALM 46

In Arthur Miller's play *Death of a Salesman* Willy Loman is a tragic, poignant, despairing figure. The salesman wants so much to be loved by his family, to be "accepted as he is." He thinks he must "wow" them by being a big success, but he still can't get close to them.

Only a glimmer of hope for Willy is seen in the play, for example, when his son Biff has protested that his father should leave his "phony dream" and admit that neither he nor his sons are leaders of men. One can sense the desire of Biff to "break through" to his father. He leaves the scene in tears.

Willy turns to his wife, Linda, and with the crashing realization of his son's real affection for him cries out: "Isn't that—isn't that remarkable? Biff—he likes me!"

A psychiatrist has said that every person needs at least one individual in his life with whom he can completely "be himself." We need acceptance, relationship, affection.

Many an individual, especially at a large university, may go begging for such a friend and such a relationship.

What a wonderful comfort it is to have the greatest Friend and Confidant of all—our blessed Lord! When others fail us or when we have no one with whom to share life's pains and joys, He is always near.

171

The beauty of it is that He likes us. He does not like our sin, nor does He overlook it. For it cost Him His life.

But us He does like, and He loves us with an everlasting love. He has declared us "acceptable" —us, the unacceptable. He loves us, the unlovable.

What a joy, no matter what difficulties the day may bring, to be able to lift up our eyes and say: "He likes me!"

And They Came Tumbling Down

READ 1 THESSALONIANS 4

A Christian student was assigned to room with another student who was not a member of the church. As he moved into his new quarters and got himself settled, he noticed that one wall of the room was covered with rather objectionable pictures which had been placed there by his new roommate.

He didn't know quite how to handle the situation, was deeply disturbed by the vulgarity and rudeness of the pictures, yet didn't want to be legalistic in his approach to the problem.

What did he do? The Christian student simply put up an artist's depiction of Christ on the same wall. Without any word being exchanged between the two students, day after day one picture after another came down off the wall until the only picture that was left was the picture of Christ.

Somehow the other pictures just did not fit in with the picture of our blessed Lord.

This is Christ's way in a person's life. There are some things which one just cannot hang onto if Christ is going to be the "chief character" in his life. The Scripture says: "Do not try to work together as equals with unbelievers, for it cannot be done. How can right and wrong be partners? How can light and darkness live together? How can Christ and the devil agree? What does a believer have in common with an unbeliever? How

can God's temple come to terms with pagan idols?
For we are the temple of the living God! As God
Himself has said:

> 'I will make My home with them and live
>   among them,
> I will be their God, and they shall be My
>   people.' "

(2 Corinthians 6:14-16 TEV)

These words have something to say not only
with respect to the "furniture" in our lives, the
things around us, but also the people with whom
we are intimately acquainted. This does not mean
that the only friends we are to have are to be
Christians; for if we did not know and live and
work and play with those outside the church, we
could never come to understand and love them
and bring Christ's message of forgiveness to
them.

But when Scripture says: "Be ye not unequally
yoked together with unbelievers" (2 Corinthians
6:14 KJV), and: "Come out from among them, and
be ye separate, saith the Lord" (2 Corinthians
6:17 KJV), it is warning us against a total identi-
fication of purpose and spirit and belief with "the
children of this world." There is a balance then
which the Christian student must always find
with God's help: to live with and love those who
do not own God as Father and Christ as their
Savior and yet to be "separate" from them as one
who follows Christ's way in everything that He
does, not the way of those who know not Christ.

The student who remains faithful to Christ,

no matter what the circumstances or relationships may be in his campus life, will find this promise of our Lord fulfilled: "I will welcome you, and I will be a Father to you, and you shall be My sons and daughters, says the Lord Almighty." (2 Corinthians 6:17-18)

READ PSALM 1

The rest of the students at the retreat were downstairs square-dancing. But this young man had pulled me aside with the tugging plea: "Have you got a minute?" And soon his story was tumbling out.

"I get so churned up inside I don't know which way to go. I was real proud of myself this year when I averaged out with a high *C* in school. Then other kids showed me their *B*'s, and my heart fell; and some of them didn't even have to try hard, and they made straight *A*'s.

"And I have to work so hard for what I get, I got real discouraged. I guess my pride was hurt. And this same bunch wanted me to go out with them on Saturday night and live it up; but I just didn't care for it. And I get so terribly lonely sitting there all alone in the dorm. I've tried to be a good Christian. *But there's no call out for good guys this semester."*

This young man had a double-barreled problem. But God in His love has help for these and any other problems that will confront him in his academic career.

First of all, Christ encourages us to be content with such things as we have—also the powers of mind and body which are a unique gift from Him to us. Oh, not that we shouldn't make the most of our abilities; but He does not expect us to be someone else. He does expect us to do our very best, by God's good grace, with such mental and physical equipment as He has given us. "It is required in stewards that a man be found faithful" (1 Corinthians 4:2 KJV). The results are up to God and to His glory.

Although there is often loneliness in campus life, also because one is leading a life of Christian integrity, Christ has promised that we will not be alone. He has assured us of a peace which the world cannot give; therefore our hearts should not be troubled nor afraid. (John 14:27)

Prayer After a Lost Weekend

READ ROMANS 6

O Lord, I'd better not pray this prayer but just once in a while — when I truly am sorry for having made such poor use of my time and wasted so many precious hours over a weekend when I knew there was so much to be done. What can I say when I have done it again and been such an unfaithful steward of all the gifts You have given me — my mind, opportunity for study at a fine school, the encouragement and support of my teachers and parents and friends?

I really don't deserve Your forgiveness, Lord, but You have said that You will never cast out anyone who comes to You with a truly penitent heart, that You will forgive me if I honestly confess my sin to You and am sincerely sorry.

I know it isn't just Your business to forgive sins, dear God; for my sins of slothfulness have also cost the death of my dear Savior, Jesus Christ. But while there is yet grace with You, as You have promised, I come humbly beseeching Your forgiveness. Give me grace now to make use of such time as I have left, and by Your Holy Spirit inspire in me the diligence to amend my sinful life. Into Your hands I commit myself, also for a night of refreshing sleep, that I might arise to do Your will.

In Christ's name I ask it. Without His help I just can't do anything. Amen.

"I Believe"

Let me tell you what I believe when I confess the faith of the Christian church in the Apostles' Creed.

I believe that God made me and everything around me. I do not believe that the world was a product of chance or of accident but that an incomprehensible, majestic, and all-wise Creator brought it into being by a divine fiat.

Oh, to be sure, I don't have all the answers as to how it happened who knows how many years ago — or in great detail how God accomplished this miracle of creation; but I do know that it happened.

I also know through the revelation of Scripture that God created man a rational being with a spirit. On these points Scripture is very clear. I know that God has also made me as part of this vast creation of all things in heaven and earth. Since I am His creation, I owe Him my whole life and know I can count on Him for His care. Thus I say, "I believe in God the Father Almighty, Maker of heaven and earth."

In the Second Article of the Creed I echo the wisdom of the Wise Men in worshiping "Jesus Christ, His only Son, Our Lord."

I believe that Jesus Christ had no human father but was born of a virgin mother by a miracle of the Holy Spirit.

I believe that Jesus Christ was a full-fledged

179

human being, was tempted even as I am tempted
—but differing from me not in degree but in
kind—suffered and died on the cross in the great
mystery of God giving Himself for man.

I further believe that Christ's resurrection
is not a mere "survival of personality beyond
the grave," like Plato or Luther or Abraham
Lincoln, but that Christ, doing the impossible,
proved His deity and fulfilled His promise of
power over the grave for us by rising from the
tomb on the third day, later ascending into
heaven, whence He shall come to judge the quick
and the dead.

Further, I believe in a real hell, not just "hell
on earth," although plenty of people make that
for themselves too. But I believe, on the authority
of the Son of God Himself, that there will be an
endless separation from God for those who have
rejected Christ as their Savior from sin. And one
of the most agonizing things about this existence
into eternity will be that such self-loving individuals will be separated forever from the God
who created them, loved them, and gave His own
life to save them from the destruction they ultimately brought upon themselves.

I believe on the other hand in a real heaven,
not a box somewhere up in the sky with gold
cobblestones and mansions reminiscent of Vic-
torian architecture but, in a dimension at present
not grasped by me, a life which in the most basic
terms means being face to face with my Maker
in a living and joyous fellowship of worship and
service which will never end.

In the Third Article I confess my faith in that Person of the Holy Trinity who has brought me into this living faith in God—the Holy Spirit. I believe in what Christ calls His church, the mystical union of all true believers, be they Methodists, Baptists, Roman Catholics, or Lutherans, wherever they hold the central teaching that Christ, the God-man, alone redeemed men from sin and that one is saved solely through faith in Him.

I therefore believe with Job: "I know that my Redeemer liveth and that He shall stand at the latter day upon the earth; and though after my skin worms destroy this body, yet in my flesh shall I see God, whom I shall see for myself and mine eyes shall behold, and not another." (Job 19:25-27 KJV)

This I believe, and this I am compelled to state as a Christian, not (as God is my witness) from any sense of false pride but because "I cannot but speak the things which I have seen and heard." (Acts 4:20 KJV)

Where Do You Go from Here?

READ HEBREWS 12

Many people still cling to the notion that their appraisal of Christianity can take place in a vacuum, that "it's something I'm going to have to think out for myself."

But God has promised that one cannot know of Him and "the things of the Spirit of God" unless he uses the tools by which He reveals Himself to man. Many a student goes on month after month sincerely pleading for a "discoverable God," yet making no real effort to use the means by which God can speak to him: His written Word, the sacraments, and the fellowship of Christians.

Where do you go from here? Now come the "commencement exercises." If you are not doing so already, begin intensive study of the Scriptures, regular participation in the Lord's Supper, and dialog with Christians who are really living their faith.

The following guidelines form a brief commentary on this process. There are no gimmicks here, no easy solutions. For every person it will be different, for each begins at a different stage of spiritual development.

But the tools are there for you to use. Leave them untouched, and nothing will happen. But let God speak to you, listen to His voice, do His will, and you shall "know the truth," know, too, that it is "of God."

1. *Search the Scriptures.* Use a modern trans-

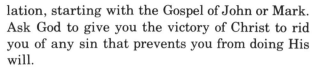

lation, starting with the Gospel of John or Mark. Ask God to give you the victory of Christ to rid you of any sin that prevents you from doing His will.

2. *Relive your Baptism every day.* Praise God for His mighty act in claiming you, an orphan, as His very own and receiving you into His royal family through this "washing of regeneration" in the blessed sacrament of Holy Baptism.

3. *Participate in the celebration of the Lord's Supper frequently.* Here is your clue and channel for an active fellowship with Christ. In the blessed Eucharist yield your whole person to your victorious Redeemer, and He will take you, penetrate you, and assimilate you to Himself.

4. *Practice private confession.* The church of the Reformation retained this practice for the great benefits it gives to the penitent. Specific sins may be confessed, or one may make a general confession in private.

5. *Prayer,* like worship, involves our total relationship with God. For specific prayers, don't forget the hymnal and the psalms. Pray with an open heart, asking that God's will be done.

6. *Live out the Christian life,* not only in association with fellow Christians but also in every other relationship and task on campus.

In this whole process depend not on yourself but on Christ. Look to "Jesus, the Pioneer and Perfecter of our faith, who for the joy that was set before Him endured the cross, despising the shame, and is seated at the right hand of the throne of God."

He is inviting you right now to a life of joy
and service inside His church.

Won't you please come on in?